Praise for

The Cocktail Hour Garden

∽

"*The Cocktail Hour Garden* reminds us that gardens are meant to be savored, and that there is no better place to enjoy the day's 'closing ceremony' than our own backyard. Let C.L. Fornari be your clever and inventive guide to creating the perfect retreat for enjoying your evening cocktail and the life around you."

~ **Amy Stewart,** *author of* The Drunken Botanist: the Plants that Create the World's Great Drinks

"C.L. Fornari explores the importance of the green hour, a time at the end of every day when the light shifts, and sounds and scents intensify. She encourages us to put down our phones, laptops, and tablets, to slow down and take a deep breath. The important thing is to appreciate this special time of day, to make a connection with the natural world and the people you share it with. And C.L. can show you how to do just that, with or without an adult beverage!"

~ **Ellen Zachos,** *author of* Backyard Foraging, *with a specialty in foraged cocktails*

"*The Cocktail Hour Garden* makes garden design festive, fun, creative, functional and easy. By looking at the landscape similar to the way we look at rooms indoors, it makes it easy to design each area of the garden for its intended purpose, whether to relax, observe nature, or enjoy a private cocktail in the twilight garden with a special friend."

~ **Ciscoe Morris,** *author, speaker and host of "Gardening With Ciscoe" on radio and television*

"What a fun concept for a book and what a great read it is! C.L Fornari invites us to join her for cocktails in the garden, where she introduces us to fun facts about all manner of subjects: plant-based drinks, crepuscular insects, evening illuminations, and scented, tactile and night-blooming plants, to name just a few. Enjoy!"

~ **Julie Moir Messervy,** *landscape designer and author of* Landscape Ideas That Work

"There are two important messages in C.L. Fornari's new book that every gardener, no matter how good, has to read. The first is to evaluate each plant for whether it's helping or hindering the enjoyment of our garden. The second is to consider whether your garden reflects your lifestyle and gives you concrete steps to create a garden that is yours. I also appreciated the specific recommendations for plants, particularly the most fragrant ones I may not have considered before."

~ **Doug Green**, DougGreensGarden.com

"C.L. Fornari has mastered the art of entertaining in the garden. In *The Cocktail Hour Garden,* she shares how delightful and magical gardens can be after hours. C.L. inspires us with practical design ideas, planting suggestions, history lessons, favorite garden memories and grow-your-own botanical cocktail recipes. Adding new perspectives to gardening, this book is for those of us who love to work, live and play in our gardens."

~ **Melissa Caughey**, of Tilly's Nest and author of A Kid's Guide to Keeping Chickens

"I love this book! C.L.Fornari sees the lawn and garden as a destination for evening parties. She gives thought-provoking suggestions for plants that deliver delicious afternoon and evening fragrance, and pays particular attention to the night-blooming colors and textures of garden plants. The basic question she asks both the reader and homeowner to answer is, 'What does this plant bring to the party?'"

~ **Jim Long**, landscape designer and author of numerous books on herbs and gardening; LongCreekHerbs.com

"When I lived in an old farmstead in the Pocono Mountains back in the '70s I remember an almost daily sunset ritual of walking through my large vegetable garden, drinking a beer and hunting aphids. It was always a magical moment. Now I do the same thing on the balcony of the Rose Tattoo, the old bar turned studio/home here in New Orleans, except it's with a martini and there is no bug hunting! C.L.'s lovely book, *The Cocktail Hour Garden,* has reinforced in me the importance of balancing the 'real world' day by acknowledging the beauty of the natural world as it's revealed in the magical evening. Good on ya, C.L., you have produced a remarkable work."

~ **Thomas Mann**, jewelry artist, designer, New Orleans

"The photos in *The Cocktail Hour Garden* remind me of why so many people go garden and plant crazy. We wish to have our own sanctuary and oasis of peace and satisfaction. For just a few minutes a day, this is our moment of equipoise."

~ **Joseph De Sciose**, Joseph De Sciose Photography

The

Cocktail Hour Garden

The

Cocktail Hour Garden

Creating Evening Landscapes for Relaxation and Entertaining

C.L. Fornari

st. lynn's
press

PITTSBURGH

The Cocktail Hour Garden
Creating Evening Landscapes for Relaxation and Entertaining

ISBN-13: 978-1-943366-02-6

Library of Congress Control Number: 2015947989.
CIP information available upon request

First Edition, 2016

St. Lynn's Press . POB 18680 . Pittsburgh, PA 15236
412.381.9933 . www.stlynnspress.com

Book design – Holly Rosborough
Editor – Catherine Dees
Editorial Intern – Christina Gregory

Photo credits:
All photos © C.L. Fornari, with the exception of:
Pgs 11, 12, 113, 132, 162 – © Holly Rosborough

Printed in China on certified FSC (Forest Stewardship Council) recycled paper using soy-based inks. This paper was sourced responsibly in a way that ensures the long-term health of forests.

This title and all of St. Lynn's Press books may be purchased for educational, business or sales promotional use. For information please write:
Special Markets Department . St. Lynn's Press . POB 18680 . Pittsburgh, PA 15236

10 9 8 7 6 5 4 3 2 1

*This book is dedicated to the natural world
in our backyards and gardens.*

❧

It's important for me to thank you because when I was a child you welcomed me completely. You let me pick your flowers, be embraced by the limbs of your trees, and hide under your bushes. You offered me glimpses into a thousand wonders. By the way, I'm sorry I squashed your yew berries and then mixed in the ants that were attracted to them. I thought the ants were icky and killing them made me feel powerful; I was just a kid and didn't know better.

Through all of my life you've provided me with opportunities for discovery and creativity. I hope you know how important this is. To be able to be constantly learning is such a blessing.

I could go on about the ways you provide all of us with good exercise, connections to other people, delicious fresh food, a place to meditate, beautiful flowers, and relaxing surroundings for coffee and cocktail hours, because all of that is valued. Running beneath and through all of those offerings are your healing forces that we don't always understand yet continually benefit from.

❧

*Every time I take the time to sit and observe the
natural world, know that I'm exceedingly grateful.
Backyards and gardens, this book is for you.*

Table of Contents

The Return of "The Green Hour"

Some say that the cocktail hour began in Paris, with the custom of pausing after the workday for a small glass of absinthe. This highly alcoholic green-hued drink – made from herbs such as wormwood, fennel and green anise – was first sold in the late 18th century as a cure-all. In the early 19th century, the potent beverage became popular as a before-dinner aperitif. So many people looked forward to sipping their glass of absinthe at this time of the evening that the period became known as *l'heure vert*, the green hour.

Although to this day I haven't tried absinthe, it's not surprising that I'm in favor of the concept of a green hour. For a gardener such as myself, green isn't the color of an intoxicating drink but the color of healthy plants. I'd estimate that the average garden would be over 80% green if we charted its component colors. Yet green also exemplifies other qualities that we hold dear.

Green can mean lush, verdant, luxuriant, fertile. It's a term for a park, playing field or neighborhood common space – or a way to describe something natural, pure, eco-friendly and organic. Green also implies freshness, or something that's young and new. Who wouldn't want a period of each day devoted to these qualities?

Whether the practice of pausing for a drink between the workday and the evening meal began with absinthe or not, I propose that the best place to celebrate a return of the green hour is among plants, in the garden. We can all use a time to pause among the surrounding greenery and count our blessings, whether it's with a cup of tea, a cocktail or no beverage in hand at all.

This break at the end of the day, and the ritual of connecting with the natural world and the people around me, was the impetus behind this book. At Poison Ivy Acres, my husband and I have a deck that overlooks the lake. Or it *would* overlook the lake, I should say, if the various shrubs, trees and other plants between the house and the water didn't prevent us from seeing most of this Cape Cod kettle pond. But lake view or not, it has become our custom to sit here every evening when the weather is conducive.

Over the many cocktail hours we've spent on this deck, I've come to appreciate that there are particular qualities that go into creating a special surrounding for this time of day. There are plants that light up in the golden rays of the setting sun and those that show up nicely in the low light after sunset; plants that release their fragrance only at night so that beginning in the cocktail hour their perfume wafts through the garden; plantings that attract birds, butterflies and other interesting wildlife, turning static surroundings into a kaleidoscope of movement, color and entertainment. All of these and more contribute to having a garden for evening enjoyment.

While writing this book, I have also come to appreciate that the least important element here is the drink that we carry into the garden. Certainly a well-made cocktail or refreshing non-alcoholic beverage adds to our pleasure, and there are plants we can include in our gardens that provide tasty drink ingredients. But the most significant aspect of this space is that it provides an environment where we intentionally stop working and connect with the greater world.

Living in this oh-so-digital 21st century, we are surrounded by labor-saving devices, yet people are working longer hours. For some, the work never stops. We carry email, text and mobile connections with us constantly as our phones have become small computers. I know couples that bring their laptops to the dinner table and into bed. I know individuals of all ages who seldom focus on the people they are actually with because their smartphone demands attention. How can we truly be where we are anymore?

The cocktail hour garden is a landscape that reminds us to put these distractions aside and be in the present moment. It's an environment that, like a strong ocean current, pulls us determinedly into the natural world and invites us to relax and better sync our rhythms to the flora and fauna around us.

This book is an invitation to come outside at the end of the day and celebrate all the ways we are truly connected. Bring your family and friends or enjoy a period of individual retreat. Create a personal green space, a cocktail hour environment for relaxation and appreciation. Once you're there, sitting in your garden, imagine that I'm nearby, lifting a glass in tribute. I propose the first toast in the book: To the return of the green hour!

C.L.

You are invited

TO:

Make a Green Hour Garden

WHERE:

In Your Yard & Garden

WHEN:

5 to 8 P.M.

RSVP:

To Relaxation and Entertainment

One

The Cocktail Hour Garden

When I conduct landscape consultations, I often ask the homeowners, "What is this plant bringing to the party?" I'm referring to landscaping that is *way* past its prime. It might be shrubs that are either half-dead or bushes that have been so repeatedly and poorly pruned that everyone wishes they *would* die, and quickly. The homeowners may have been reluctant to remove such specimens before, because, "It's still got some life in it," or "Maybe it will come back."

But when I compare the landscape to a festive gathering and ask what these particular specimens are contributing, the homeowners can see their plants with new eyes. It helps that the question is about the plant's contribution to the landscape, rather than the gardener's reason for keeping it. If I ask, "What does this bring to the party?" the answer is likely to be, "Not much." Although we're not, thank goodness, focusing on failing plants in this book, I nevertheless have a similar goal. I want readers to see their yards and gardens from a new, celebratory perspective.

My focus here is on creating landscapes for evening relaxation, renewal and entertaining, so the party metaphor is fitting. When planning festive gatherings, we decide who will be invited and where the event will take place. Plans are made for the menu and decorations. We address questions about the theme and the occasion being celebrated and pay attention to how all aspects of the surroundings can enhance the partygoers' experience.

Come into the evening garden as often as you can. Even in the cool spring, crispy fall or dead of winter, it's relaxing to reconnect with the natural world at the end of the day.

Arranging a party is a creative act; it's a matter of combining several elements to make something larger that is pleasing to the senses. And, like a party, the final outcome is unknowable. Will the end product be enjoyable? Might someone get wild and dance on the tables or flirt outrageously with the host? Could the plants be crazy-beautiful, seducing everyone who enters the garden? Will something magical happen? At a party or in a garden, anything is possible, and the planning is part of the fun.

Changing Landscapes

When I think about it, the landscapes around our homes haven't changed much since the 1960s. Isn't it strange that car, clothing and hair styles are completely different than they were in 1965 (*thankfully*, some would say, when recalling the hair-sprayed flips that many women wore) – yet the front yards of all my childhood homes still look pretty much the same as they did in that era. Yikes! Our front and backyards are wearing outdated hairdos!

It's time for a much-needed makeover. So, let's consider the landscape not as that collection of random plants that surrounds the house, but as your own personal party venue. Your yard can be the setting for a series of celebrations, large and small, daily or occasional: sitting alone with a cup of coffee and noticing that the first flower has opened on one of your perennials, gathering with friends around the fire pit to toast the beginning or end of summer or sitting companionably with your spouse on the patio at dusk. All of these may not call for party hats and paper lanterns, but they are indeed small celebrations of life.

Anyone can have a yard that's primarily green space; most houses come with such landscapes already in place, and most people dutifully tend them. But why not have a yard that draws you outdoors in your down time? Why not think of your landscape as a place that enriches the other facets of your life – as an extension of your home?

Indoors, we know that people sleep in bedrooms, cook in kitchens and bathe in the bathroom. We have favorite places to read, watch television or work on the computer. Why not view the garden the same way? Here is the part of the yard where we sit with our morning coffee. There is the space for reading or

Different strokes for different folks! Just as people prefer varying styles of footwear, they also favor differing types of gardens. Growing veggies and ornamental plants in Smart Pots is perfect for some but not for others. There isn't just one way to garden.

Most gardens have a sense of place, and this patio in Umbria is no exception. But there are take-home design principles that can translate to any location. 1) A mass of one color is always impressive. Here, the coral red is repeated in all of the flowers, and it ties the plantings in with the red tones in the stonework and walls. 2) Going up is important. Gardens should have vertical elements, and if that can't be a tree or tall shrub, vines on a framework will work just as well. 3) A combination of formal and informal works nicely in small gardens. The sheared, formal shape of the topiary on the corner is offset by the loose growth habit of the trumpet vine.

writing. This part of the landscape is where the kids build their forts and that garden is filled with flowers for creating give-away bouquets. This garden is for reflection or napping, and that one for entertaining.

Seen with these eyes, our gardens become a series of outdoor living spaces. We plant the Breakfast Garden, Outdoor Office, Play Yard, Meditation Garden and Party Patio. Instead of the green window dressing that's placed around our yards out of tradition and habit, what we could actually have is a series of outdoor rooms that enhance daily living.

And one or more of those spaces can be the Cocktail Hour Garden, the perfect location to observe the green hour.

The umbrella hints at the destination that will be reached once you start down the paths in Maria Nation's garden. Umbrellas are a natural way to accent the cocktail hour garden, not because shade is needed during the evening hours but because they symbolize shelter.

A Toast To...
Newly-Purposed Garden Sheds

In days gone by, the buildings outside of a home might commonly be a barn, an outhouse or assorted chicken coops and pigpens. Today's suburban and urban yards are more likely to contain small storage sheds, gazebos or pool houses. Recently we've seen a trend that brings the man cave outdoors and blends the cocktail hour garden with the traditional garden shed. Give a warm welcome to the bar shed.

Although the fake-palm-covered tiki-bar has been an accepted fixture in mobile home parks and other vacation homes, it seems that the traditional garden shed is moving into this territory. From the outside, these structures look like the normal outbuildings that hold tools, pots and other gardening supplies. Open the large doors, however, and you'll find glasses, a wide assortment of beverages and possibly sinks or small refrigerators.

Some bar sheds are even large enough to hold a bistro table and chairs, while others have the customary stools and tall counter. These structures might be placed near a pool or water feature, open onto a patio or be surrounded by privacy-screening plants.

Sheds have frequently been repurposed in yards and gardens when homeowners, looking for extra space, have cleared out the tools and created places for reading, writing or potting up plants. Those with larger outbuildings have installed screens on the windows or mosquito netting drapes and turned these outbuildings into sleeping rooms.

Beyond the daylilies and the white flowering Persicaria polymorpha *at Good Dogs Farm is a shed that's reserved for sleeping. To go to sleep serenaded by the crickets and frogs and wake up to birdsong at dawn is magical in itself. This shed, surrounded by the exquisite gardens created by Maria Nation, is a most enchanted outbuilding.*

A friend of mine has such a shed and says that being able to sleep and wake up without hearing the refrigerator running or seeing the tiny lights of computers, clocks and televisions is wonderful. "All we can hear is the birds singing, and it's just magical," he told me.

The garden shed can be anything your imagination wants it to be.

So I propose a toast: to outbuildings that are defined not by tradition, but by the needs and fancy of their owners.

7

Marking Transitions:
rituals and re-connections

Humans have long marked the big changes in our lives. Many cultures and religious traditions have rituals for passing from a child into to adulthood, for example. At weddings, we celebrate going from being single to beginning a partnership and new family with another adult. We pause to commemorate events that are joyous, bittersweet and sad as we observe the birth of babies, retirement from a long career and deaths.

We have customs for the smaller occasions in life as well. From daily prayers before a meal to the cups of coffee served at the start of a board meeting, we regularly observe many routines and circumstances throughout our days. One of those regular rituals has been the cocktail hour.

Most accounts of the history of the cocktail list the 19th century as the period when it all began, and they define the beverage as a mixed drink. I have found a reference in an 1882 edition of Punch that refers to "Champagne-cocktail-hour" at 1 p.m., followed, para-doxically, by "Coffee-and-liqueur" at 3 p.m. I guess in the late 19th century they didn't share the current thinking that mixing caffeine and alcohol isn't a very good idea.

But, be it a mixed cocktail, a mug of beer or a cup of tea, pausing in the evening with a beverage clearly has a long tradition. I can find little mention of that practice being done outdoors, however. The focus has been on the beverage, the traditions or equip-ment for mixing drinks, and what the glass contains rather than on the surroundings where the ritual takes place. I'd like to suggest that these two should go hand in hand...or glass in hand in garden, to be more specific.

When staged outdoors in a natural environment, the cocktail hour is more than a transition from the workday into the dinner hour. It is the time to mark a shift from human pursuits and general business to a period where we acknowledge and appreciate our connectedness to the world around us. For most people, their daily work is indoors and cut off from nature. The cocktail hour garden functions to gently shift our focus to the greater world where we live and the wonder of the plants that sustain all life.

During the evening hours, the natural world is in transition as well. Animals that hunt and eat during the day seek those places where can they take cover for the night. But as the wildlife that's on the "day shift" hunkers down, the nocturnal hunters or grazers begin their workday...or, more accurately, work night. For the owls, beavers, coyotes, skunks or others, the evening hours are when a host of animals and insects wake up and get on the move. Some of these are visible in our gardens, and seeing them adds to our appreciation of the connectedness of every-thing in the natural world and the daily transitions we pass through or celebrate.

At Dreamflower Garden in Arizona, Lorien Tersey says they use this chili-light festooned area daily. *"The porch opens into our living room, so when we have parties and potlucks we open up the double doors and people spill out of the house onto the porch, with music and food and drinks. Sometimes the bats hunt insects at the lights above us. Facing west, the porch gives us a beautiful view of the sky at sunset and is a wonderful place to watch the monsoon storms in the summer without getting wet."*

A Garden For the Senses

The twilight garden is truly sensational in all defini-
tions of the word. In the cocktail hour garden, all of
our senses (smell, taste, sight, touch, hearing) can be
engaged if we've designed diversely planted spaces
that are welcoming to people and wildlife.

The plants in this container all beg to be touched. The thin, soft
blades of the Mexican feather grass *(Nassella tenuissima)* contrast
with the hard waxy spirals of the corkscrew rush *(Juncus effusus
'Curly Wurly')* and the scrub brush-like Pink Zazzle™ globe amaranth
(Gomphrena hybrid).

Smell, taste and sight will be explored at length
in later chapters. But for the moment, consider
the senses of touch and hearing and how these are
present in the cocktail hour garden.

TOUCH: There are some plants that just beg to
be petted. Some plants are so soft and fuzzy that it's
impossible to resist reaching out to touch
the leaves. Many grasses have such fine
or silky blades that they invite stroking,
much as we are compelled to run our
hands though the soft fur of a cat or dog.

Some flowers look like velvet or have
such a chenille-like appearance that we
just have to handle their petals. Annual
celosia and many petunia flowers have a
velvety texture that draws us nearer and
practically insists on being rubbed. Even
plants with very smooth foliage can be
interesting and compelling to feel when
they are close at hand.

When planting containers for the
cocktail hour garden, it's worthwhile to
include several sensory plant varieties
that invite us to touch as well as see and
smell. Because pots and boxes can be
placed near where we sit, using a range
of pettable plants in these containers
enriches our enjoyment in the evening
landscape.

Plants That Invite Our Touch

Here are a few plants that you just have to handle.

COCKSCOMB CELOSIA *(Celosia cristata)*

These flowers look like someone took red, orange or yellow velvet and crinkled up the fabric into a bunch that looks sort of brain-like. The flowers are both soft and brilliant. Whether you plant them in pots or in the ground, grow these in full sun and well-drained soil.

FIBER OPTIC GRASS *(Isolepsis cernua aka Scirpus cernuus)*

This bright green annual sedge makes most people smile as they run their hands over the tiny cream-colored flowers that appear at the ends of the leaves. If you place this in a pot with other plants, be sure to select companions that also like constantly moist soil; fiber optic grass likes it wet.

'FLAMINGO FEATHER' *(Celosia spicata 'Flamingo Feather')*

Picture a thick, pointed pipe cleaner that's been dipped into pink dye, and you'll come close to this annual plant. Its brilliant pink plumes are so soft and fuzzy looking that it's hard not to imagine that they are paintbrushes used to color brilliant pink flamingo lawn ornaments.

Flamingo Feather has brilliant pink plumes.

FLAPJACK PLANT *(Kalanchoe thyrsiflora)*

This plant is touchable not because it's fuzzy or silky, but because it's so smooth and unplant-like. You'd almost think that this sculptural kalanchoe has been designed by an artist and molded from plastic. Plant this for a modern look or place it in planters that may not be watered frequently.

LAMB'S EAR *(Stachys byzantina)*

The soft velvety leaves of lamb's ear are impossible to resist. Although this plant is usually grown as a groundcover or mixed into a perennial garden, it can be both attractive and perennial in a large box or other container. Cultivars such as 'Cotton Boll', 'Big Ears' and 'Wave Hill' have slightly larger leaves than the species and received good performance ratings in a comparative study at the Chicago Botanic Garden.

NASTURTIUM *(Nasturtium hybrids* and species)

The smooth, round nasturtium leaves are compelling because they are flat and a bit silky. This foliage is a lovely combination of stylish and serviceable, and for this reason it invites our touch. Recent rain or irrigation adds to the charm by displaying diamond-like drops of water on each leaf, as lovingly displayed as a jewel in the cases at Tiffany & Co.

SILVER SAGE *(Salvia argentea)*

Although this sage does flower, most people grow it for the large, silver, fuzz-coated leaves. The crinkled, wavy foliage covered with white down provides so much appeal that blossoming is almost beside the point. This sage is said to be perennial in zones 5 to 10, but most gardeners in the colder regions find it to be a tender biennial at best. Plant it as an annual, and if it comes back in subsequent years, think of it as a gift from God.

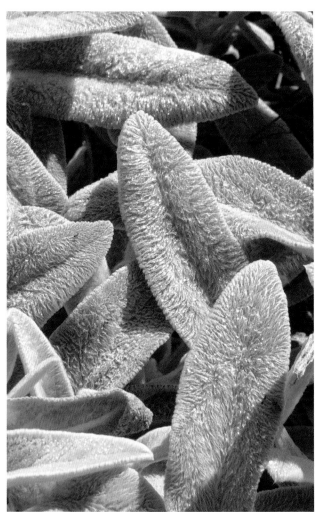

Velvety Lamb's Ear leaves are impossible to resist.

HEARING: While we experience the sensation of feeling many textures with our fingertips, we are also aware of the levels of sound that surround the cocktail hour garden. Birdcalls, tree frogs, crickets and cicadas are just a few of the critters that serenade us in the evening hours.

Perhaps add man-made harmonies into the chorus by hanging bells or wind chimes in the garden or by installing fountains that spray or drip water. Or, use outdoor speakers to bring recorded music into the landscape. All of these options are especially appealing in areas where traffic noise or sounds from neighboring houses need to be masked.

Think of the process of designing a cocktail hour garden as the layering of experiences for the senses so that your whole body becomes involved. When we are called by smell, taste, sight, touch and hearing, the experience of the green hour becomes a complex, full-immersion encounter.

There is something soothing about just looking at a pair of rocking chairs placed in a garden. The Chapmans' garden in Falmouth, MA, is practically a recipe for a relaxing landscape. Take two rocking chairs, add a patio, mix in a variety of foliage textures and sprinkle with a smattering of flowers. Enjoy with the beverage of your choice!

Just For Fun...
Cocktail Hour Blossoming

● There are some plants that only flower from the cocktail hour on into the night. Typically, these are blooms that attract pollinators with their scents, and often, the flowers are white. The perfume of such flowers draws evening and night-flying insects in, and the light petals make a more visible landing pad. Annuals with flowers that open during the cocktail hour include moonflower *(Ipomoea alba)*, flowering tobacco *(Nicotiana alata)*, and four o'clocks *(Mirabilis jalapa)*.

● Cause for many cocktail hour celebrations, the night blooming cereus has fragrant white flowers that open in the evening and are wilting by the next morning. Although that common name is used for many evening-flowering plants, the most widely grown night blooming plant is *Epiphyllum oxypetalum*, also known as Dutchman's pipe cactus or queen of the night. Because some people wait for several years for this epiphyte to start flowering, it's no wonder that impromptu parties are held when the flowers open.

Although the common name for Mirabilis jalapa *is four o'clocks, you wouldn't want to set your watch by these flowers. Instead, consider these colorful trumpets that herald the coming of night sometime during the evening hours. The flowers that entertain your cocktail hour will also be there before dawn, so you can sip your morning coffee in their cheerful company.*

A Garden For the Mind

The cocktail hour garden is not just a feast for the senses...it's also a banquet for the mind. Whenever we pause to be fully present in the natural world, we can't help but notice things that cause us to wonder. As we question what we smell, taste, see, touch and hear, we're presented with opportunities to learn about the garden and the other beings that we share these spaces with.

Why is that bird pouncing on the ground again and again? Is it seeking food or a mate? How did the group of yellow daylilies we planted five years ago suddenly contain an orange flowering plant with double petals? And why does one plant drop its leaves after sundown while another keeps its foliage in the same position day and night?

Even the ritual of sitting with open eyes in the same place around the same period each day allows us to connect to the natural world in a deeper way. We may notice that particular animals pass through the yard at the same time each evening or be able to notice from one week to the next a change in the angle of the setting sun or duration of daylight. Being present for even a brief time, willing to experience the connectedness of all the garden's inhabitants, can be as stimulating to the intellect as it is soothing to body and soul.

The cocktail hour garden is the perfect place to play with color and form. It is a three-dimensional collage where an assortment of plants, furniture and accent structures can be arranged and rearranged according to your whims and creativity. In this Hudson Valley garden belonging to Bernie and Lydia Kukoff, Lydia has used an artist's eye to make an evening space filled with assorted vintage porch furniture. "If there were such a category as a perfect cocktail-hour garden," Lydia writes, "this would be it."

Right Plant/Person/Place

Garden geeks are fond of talking about right plant/right place. This is shorthand for growing a plant in the environment where it is not only most likely to thrive but also least likely to do any harm. Placing a sun-loving sedum in deep shade will cause that perennial to sulk or die, for example. Similarly, it makes no sense to put a plant that loves good drainage and soils on the dry side into the yard's boggy spot.

A fragrant gardenia and *Brugmansia* add to the ambiance created by the warm color of the nearly 200 year-old brick building. The owner of this beautiful patio at Newington in Sewickley, PA, suggests that the most appropriate drink for this post-Colonial setting would be a hard apple cider.

We also recognize that our plant choices have an effect on local ecosystems, so homeowners and gardeners are increasingly careful not to make choices that will overrun the neighborhood and choke out native plants and wildlife. Knowing that plants that seldom spread or seed in one part of the country can be invasive in another region gives us an additional understanding of right plant/right place.

In the design of our gardens, we not only think about placing plants in the perfect location, we consider our own needs as well. Whether it's a desire for less mowing, more shade or fresh vegetables, we become matchmakers who pair the right plant with the perfect place along with the needs of the people involved.

When designing the cocktail hour garden, we therefore consider all aspects of this green hour setting. In this way, the planning and planting of these outdoor rooms becomes a process of weaving together our wishes, the plant's requirements and our responsibility as stewards of the environment. Add to that mix some luck and the whims and requirements of Mother Nature, and you've got a rich tapestry that is woven over time and is often as mysterious as it is beautiful. It's a process to savor and to toast at the end of the day.

Party Planning:
A Recipe for Cocktail Hour Garden Success

● Creating a garden is like any other journey: you start where you are. Find those areas in your yard that are already appealing or conducive for sitting in the evenings. A deck, patio or porch is an obvious place to begin a cocktail hour garden, but other spaces on your property might call to you as well.

● One key element in a cocktail hour garden is seating. You have to relax, right? An area where four or more people can sit is essential if you plan to entertain guests, but smaller, private spaces where one or two people can settle are also easy to transform into outdoor twilight rooms. Spend a few evenings sitting in your potential cocktail hour garden and notice what's already there that you can build on. What do you see, hear and smell? Are there views that can be enhanced or things that need to be blocked by screening? Will this area have enough space for your family and friends?

● If there isn't some sort of "flooring" in the place where you're creating a cocktail hour garden, decide if you'd like something. Although furniture can always be placed on turf, mowing such areas becomes difficult. Flat patio stones, gravel or mulch are typical bases for furniture in a garden. The decision about which flooring material to use is made by considering function, appearance and budget.

● Although a cocktail hour garden can be created some distance from the house, you're more apt to use the area frequently if it's convenient. Site your evening landscape where it's close enough to easily carry a tray of drinks and snacks outdoors. If that initial garden proves to be frequently used and you want to create others, it's always possible to venture further out into the yard from there.

● When looking at existing plants, ask yourself this: "What does this bring to the party?" If the answer is "Not much," thank it for coming and say goodbye.

● Use the other chapters in this book to add step-by-step the elements to your garden that will make it a special spot for your green hour.

The floor of this Arizona garden is carpeted, and the creator of this space at Dreamflower Garden says this isn't unusual. "Pieces of rug or carpet are not unheard of in gardens here in the desert," Lorien Tersey, explains. "They are readily available at thrift stores and yard sales or can be picked up free when the city is doing its brush and bulky pickup days. It helps reduce dust and is a nice alternative to lawn."

Seating doesn't always have to be on chairs; for a party gathering extra seating can be on a raised area like the one here.

You are invited

TO:

Be Transported by Scent

WHERE:

In Your Yard & Garden

WHEN:

5 to 8 P.M.

RSVP:

To Perfumed Breezes

Two

Fragrance

*F*ragrance is an extremely important component of the cocktail hour garden, yet it's not usually the first thing people think of when planning a landscape. We tend to focus on what we see before we put attention to what we smell – but when it comes to creating an evening garden, fragrant plants should be the first invitees on the guest list.

The Importance of Scent

Several years ago, I drove to Connecticut to visit a wholesale perennial grower. I was with my friends Roberta and Debra, who are fellow garden geeks. After a day spent at the grower's fields and green-houses, we were supposed to stop for

'Summer Fragrance' *Hosta* will brighten shady areas of the garden, and when planted near your evening festivities, the flowers scent the air, adding to the celebration of the senses.

One of the best perennials for fragrance is *Actaea simplex* 'Brunette'. The perfume from this lovely plant is noticeable from several feet away without being overpowering or too sweet. The stems that hold pinkish-white blossoms are sturdy enough to support the small birds that land there, and the flowers attract pollinators such as bumblebees.

a visit in the owner's personal garden. It was a hot August day, however, and by the time our farm tours were over, I was only thinking about getting into my air-conditioned car and driving home.

Deb and Roberta wanted to visit the private garden, so I stifled my irritability as we pulled into the driveway, got out of the car and began walking around the property. Strolling around a group of plants in the side yard, I stopped dead in my tracks. A sweet, delicious perfume was in the air, and it quickly erased my thoughts of heat and cranky fatigue. "Roberta! Deb!" I called. "What am I smelling?"

My friends looked around the garden a minute before one of them identified the plant: *Actaea simplex* 'Brunette'. Actually, what she said was "*Cimicifuga* 'Brunette'," but in the years since, this perennial's name has been changed. (A quick aside to say that maybe this name change is for the better. I remember all the times when I was working in the perennial section of the garden center and would mention *Cimicifuga*…my boss at the time would always respond with "Gesundheit!") But whether you call it *Actaea*, *Cimicifuga*, or its common name of bugbane, the flower's fragrance is powerful.

My first whiff of this plant's perfume washed away the heat and fatigue from the day. Everything else faded as I savored the sweet scent. This is the power that our sense of smell has. Pleasant odors have the ability to transport us; we can be carried back in time as a smell triggers memories, or moved away from current moods and conditions.

A Matter of Degree

"There's fragrance, and then there's *horticultural* fragrance." That's what a plant breeder remarked at a recent conference I attended, and the audience of plant professionals laughed knowingly. There are many flowers that can accurately be described as being fragrant if you stick your nose right into the blossom and inhale deeply. This is horticultural fragrance, a perfume that's present but not predominant. Such scents aren't usually powerful enough to be detected by the average human more than a foot from the bloom. The flowers may be accurately called fragrant on plant tags and in catalog listings, but they aren't likely to perfume your garden party.

Fragrance you can inhale from a distance is another matter altogether. For the cocktail hour garden, we want a surprising, sweep-me-away experience like I had when encountering *Actaea simplex* 'Brunette' for the first time. We desire plants with sweet scents that are strong enough to be perceptible without having to compete up close and personal with the bumblebees.

By the same token, though, there are some party guests who anoint themselves with far too much scent, and this makes everyone else uncomfortable. Some plants are so unrestrained when it comes to their flowers' fragrance that it is overwhelming. Scent should carry us into another dimension with gentle currents of sweet smells, not a tidal wave of robust odor.

Plants with very strong fragrances also tend to be polarizing; some people love them, while the same scent causes others to gag. The yellow flowering

The fragrance from this honeysuckle is a welcome addition to any cocktail garden.

Scotch broom, *Cytisus scoparius*, is a good example of a flowering plant that people either love or hate. If a flower's strong smell has been commonly known to cause migraines, I wouldn't recommend inviting it to the party.

Begin with Sweet Perennials, Shrubs and Vines

When designing the cocktail hour garden for fragrance, begin by including perennials and shrubs that will provide scent to your garden year after year. Plants chosen for fragrance should be sited close to the area where you'll be sitting, while plants chosen for other characteristics such as flower color or the ability to make a privacy screen can be placed throughout the yard.

Here are some fragrant plants that you might choose to invite to your cocktail hour party.

When a clove currant *(Ribes odoratum)* is planted near the cocktail hour garden, it's a double treat. The pale yellow flowers catch the rays of the setting sun and perfume the entire garden with their spicy fragrance. Note that some states have bans on various *Ribes* species, because they are an alternate host for white pine blister rust.

BANANA SHRUB *(Michelia figo)*
Zones 7-10

Fans of daiquiris or smoothies will want to have this plant for the banana-like scent of the creamy-white flowers. But beyond the fragrance, this shrub brings other benefits to your cocktail hour gathering. *Michelia figo* thrives in part sun to part shade, is tolerant of urban conditions and can either be pruned as a shrub or limbed up into a multi-stemmed small tree. This isn't a fast growing plant, but it will eventually provide some privacy screening for decks or patios, and birds will appreciate perching in its open structure on their way to feeders and birdbaths.

CLOVE CURRANT *(Ribes odoratum)*
Zones 4-8

If you could cross a yellow flowering shrub with your spice rack, you'd most likely grow the clove currant. When in flower, the aroma from this plant will have you dreaming of gingerbread or spice cookies. Although it's not the tidiest shrub on the block, and its suckering nature means you'll have to occasionally clip out wandering stems, *Ribes odoratum* is worth growing for its delicious spring perfume. Since it only grows to about four feet high, the plant is easily paired with summer-flowering shrubs. Such combinations will draw attention later in the season when the clove currant is decent enough but not spectacular. Plan on holding a spice-themed cocktail hour gathering when this *Ribes* is in bloom.

DECIDUOUS AZALEAS (*Rhododendron viscosum* and hybrids) Zones 4-9

Unlike the common spring flowering azaleas, there are many deciduous plants that flower later and are also highly fragrant. 'Weston's Lemon Drop', for example, blooms pale yellow in July, making this plant one of my top picks for the summer evening garden. Deciduous azaleas can be sheared right after flowering if you like a neat and tidy ball shape, or you can just randomly pinch the new growth to encourage a natural but full and bushy appearance. The perfume from these shrubs is reason enough to plant them, but if you want the plants to do double duty, string them with tiny white lights for some late-summer-through-winter drama. Look for other great crosses with pink flowers, such as 'Lollipop' and 'Pink and Sweet'.

DAPHNE (*Daphne* spp.) Zone hardiness varies with variety

Think of a *Daphne* as a love affair plant. When things are going well between the two of you, it will be thrilling, and that alone will be enough. But, like any love affair, it might not be very long lasting. *Daphnes* can break your heart, first with how wonderful their flowers smell, and secondly when they leave you. If you want the relationship to last as long as possible, plant them in places with excellent drainage. If your soil is on the heavy side, be sure to place them on a slope. I've had the longest relationship with *Daphne* x *transatlantica* 'Summer Ice', a variegated variety that's in flower from early summer well into the fall. For such heady scents and long lasting flowers, I'm willing to periodically get a new plant should my Daphne decide that it's time to break up.

GARDENIA (*Gardenia jasminoides*) Zones 8-10 (maybe a warm 7)

Gardenias are one of the A-list party guests that everyone wants at their cocktail hour event. The perfume of the gardenia gives northern gardeners a case of pure, soul-robbing jealousy, and many of us try to assuage our zone-envy by growing them indoors in pots. But whether they're grown in containers or in the ground, these shrubs like high humidity, bright light and soil that is reliably moist. Be sure not to plant them too deeply and know that gardenias like their personal space, so don't crowd them. Look for the fragrant 'Veitchii' and 'White Gem' if you need shorter plants, and 'August Beauty' for taller growth. All do well in pots, provided they are fertilized frequently and not allowed to dry out. In other words, give them the attention that an A-list celebrity expects.

BELGICA HONEYSUCKLE *(Lonicera periclymenum* 'Belgica') Zones 4-9 and maybe colder

Most people can think of an individual that they'd like to have at a party, while they'd prefer not to invite that person's relatives. For me, this *Lonicera* is just such a guest. There are many other honeysuckles, but because of short flowering, self-seeding, a tendency to develop mildew or (horrors!) a lack of fragrance, those relatives just aren't welcome at my cocktail hour. 'Belgica' has a fragrance that will not only fill a garden but will scent any nearby room through an open window. A vigorous grower whose tangle of branches will also shelter nesting and overwintering birds, this vine can be pruned in the spring when necessary. Deadheading will stimulate the continual flowers that attract hummingbirds. Although I'm sure that there are other family members that are similar to this woodbine, this is the plant I've known to be consistently enjoyable company.

COMMON JASMINE *(Jasminum officinale)* Zones 7-10

There are many plants that we call jasmine, and the important thing to know is that not all of them are fragrant. Common jasmine is one of the sweetly scented types with long stems that can be grown as a vine or regularly cut short. Best of all, there are varieties that come to your cocktail hour in fancy outfits. 'Affine' has maroon new growth, 'Argenteovariegatum' is variegated cream and sage green, and 'Fiona's Sunrise' has golden leaves. And what would a party be without that total extravert that makes the gathering lively? *Jasminum officinale* 'Grandiflorum' is that livewire plant, with robust growth and huge clusters of perfumed flowers.

MOONFLOWER *(Ipomoea alba)* Zones 10-12

Ah, the romantic moonflower. How can you have an evening celebration without it? During the day, this *Ipomoea's* swirled buds remain closed tight, but come evening they become twirling, flamboyant dancers, whose circle skirts open into magical white spheres. To add to the drama, the flowers display an impression of a five-pointed star. Perfumed dancers on a starry night...if you have full sun, how can you not grow this showy, annual vine?

BRUNETTE BUGBANE (*Actaea simplex* 'Brunette') Zones 3-8

You've already read how my love affair with 'Brunette' began, but here are a few more reasons you'll want to grow this perennial in your part sun/part shade garden party. This plant arrives in a suitably dark outfit that can pass for formal attire in any flowerbed. And you've heard the saying that you can't be too rich or too thin? Well, I don't know how much 'Brunette' has in the bank, but the skinny nature of its stems is definitely desirable in the garden. The tall, thin flower spikes don't dominate or shadow other plants, and they allow a view of the landscape beyond. In my garden, these stems are also frequent perching places for small birds. Add to all of this the stop-in-your-tracks fragrance, and you have a party guest that should be on nearly everyone's invitation list.

HOSTA 'SUMMER FRAGRANCE' (*Hosta* hybrids) Zones 2-9

Some party guests are just so reliably fabulous that we start to take them for granted. Such is the case for plants in the genus *Hosta*. Being such dependable, weed-smothering and shade tolerant perennials, *Hosta* cultivars are so ubiquitously planted that we expect to see them at every garden gathering. Just because they are universally valued doesn't mean you should presume that these are common, background plants. Some varieties bring fragrance to the party along with all of their other attributes. Look for 'Royal Standard', 'Fragrant Bouquet' and 'Guacamole', as well as other scented varieties.

There are some plants that are always on the garden party guest list, because they are such dependable friends. *Hosta* is just such a plant, and the variety 'Summer Fragrance' is not only reliable and well dressed, but in mid-summer arrives sporting flowers that exude a sweet, delicate perfume.

LAVENDER *(Lavendula* spp.) Zones 5-10 depending on variety

When planning a celebratory gathering, there are usually a few people who are always included. Treasured friends, beloved family members or reliably entertaining work mates will fall into the "Of course we'll be inviting..." category on the guest list. Lavender is just such a plant. The genus *Lavendula* is loved throughout the world, and many equate lavender's fragrance with relaxation. If your cocktail hour garden gets at least six hours of dead-on sun, this is a plant that you almost have to include in the beds or containers. And like the party guest that will automatically pitch in when it comes time to pass hors d'oeuvres or round up used glasses, lavender is also willing go the extra mile to make a celebration work. *Lavendula* flowers are both edible and decorative. They can be used in desserts, cocktails or savory treats and are equally at home in a bouquet or tucked into buttonholes or hair clips.

ORIENTAL LILIES *(Lilium* hybrids) Zones 3-9 depending on variety

An oriental lily is the guest you can count on to be impeccably and stylishly dressed, so we tend to be forgiving if she arrives wearing just a little too much perfume. Her heady scent is delicious, however, and also first class, so how can we complain that our dear lily has a tendency to overdo it? When including oriental lily hybrids in your garden, look for varieties that come into flower at different times in the summer so that the fragrance isn't overpowering

during one particular month. There are lists online for extending the lily blooming season. Lilies also have the advantage of being relatively thin, so they are good mixers and can be tucked among other plants in gardens and containers.

When oriental lilies are in bloom, the scent travels throughout the garden. These flowers are especially striking when planted in clusters, as Nancy Walsh did in this garden.

SWEET ALYSSUM (*Lobularia maritima*)

This low, sweet plant is an annual that you don't have to think twice about. It is the cocktail hour garden's no-brainer. Whether you scatter seeds of the reliable classic 'Carpet of Snow' or buy plants of the new, longer-lasting varieties such as Snow Princess®, the sweetly scented white flowers are the guests that you can always count on to socialize well with others. Don't hesitate to encourage seeded varieties to freshen up mid-party by giving the plant a trim. Although the new, vegetatively propagated varieties such as 'Snow Princess' don't require a haircut, plants grown from seed will benefit from snipping them back by a third when flowering starts to diminish. The Proven Winners company lists 'Snow Princess' as possibly being perennial in Zones 9-11.

TUBEROSE
(*Polianthes tuberosa*)

Here is a bulb that arrives wearing the scents of exotic, warm climates. It's no wonder that many perfumes include tuberose notes in their formulas. If you live in zones 8-10, these oh-so-fragrant party guests will be perennial, but the rest of us can enjoy *Polianthes tuberosa* by growing these bulbs as annuals. An easy way to invite tuberose notes to your cocktail hour gatherings is by planting a few bulbs in your mixed containers or in between other plants in the flowerbeds.

The bright, white Snow Princess *Lobularia* mingles beautifully with other cocktail hour guests, be it in containers or tucked into the perennial garden. In this flower-filled gathering, the *Lobularia* grows next to lavender plants, Profusion zinnias and a cloud of *Calamintha nepetoides* flowers.

VIRGINIA STOCK *(Malcolmia maritima)*

We've all heard the saying that books shouldn't be judged by their covers. Likewise, party guests shouldn't be judged by their demure, diminutive appearance. Virginia stock flowers may be small, but these tiny purple blooms put out a powerful scent.

Such reserved and modest partygoers are often the first to tire and go home, however, and this annual is no exception. Expect it to be most fragrant and colorful early in the summer but to leave the festivities when the temperatures get too warm. Virginia stock is a short-lived annual in all zones.

If your garden is in full sun and has well-drained soil, Virginia stock *(Malcolmia maritima)* will grow happily and often self-seed. Be on the lookout for young plants and remove any nearby weeds that try to crash the party.

Just For Fun...
Make a Lavender Wand

These are enjoyable to make and can be given as party favors or remembrances of a special occasion. You could even make thin ones to use as swizzle sticks!

YOU NEED:

- 5 to 11 freshly picked lavender stalks, about eight inches long (dried won't be flexible enough)
- Two yards of ribbon or flat cord between $\frac{1}{16}$ to ¼ inch wide. (The wider the ribbon, the less you'll need.)

Group the lavender stems together, with the bottom of all the flowers evenly held together. Tie one end of the ribbon around the stems at the base of the flowers and tie a tight knot.

Bend the stems back over the flowers and bring the ribbon out from the grouping.

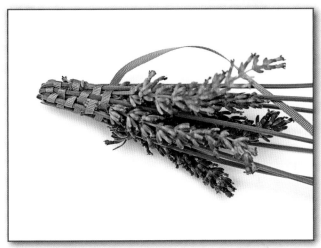

Weave the ribbon over and under the stems, pushing it up tight against the edge of the ribbon above and working around and around the wand to fully enclose the flowers in ribbon or cord.

When you begin to reach the bottom of the flowers, tighten the ribbon so that the stems are being pulled in together.

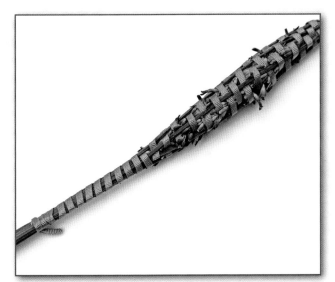

When it becomes difficult to weave, begin to wrap the ribbon around the stems for two or three inches before tying it off, leaving a few inches of ribbon hanging down.

Use another piece of ribbon to make a bow, covering the end knot and cutting the bow's ends to match the length of the other ribbon.

Fragrant Foliage

Flowers aren't the only plants that bring fragrance to the party. There are many trees, shrubs, annuals and perennials that can supply pleasing but more subtle scents in the garden. Such foliage fragrance is most abundant when the plants' oils are released by crushing needles and leaves or because of favorable weather conditions. The right levels of humidity, a recent rainfall, very warm temperatures and a lack of wind all contribute to the scents of foliage hovering in the air.

A few examples of plants with fragrant foliage: Firs (*Abies* sp.), gum trees (*Eucalyptus*), hummingbird mint (*Agastache*), and wormwood or sagebrush (*Artemisia*).

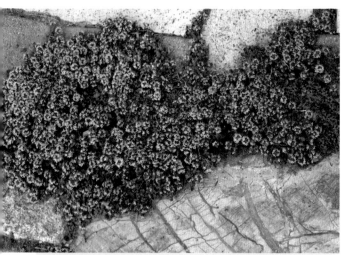

Plant creeping thyme if you'd like a carpet that is fragrant when you walk on it. There are some varieties of this herb that are especially low to the ground. For a fragrant flooring, look for elfin thyme (*T. serpyllum* 'Elfin'), wooly thyme (*T. pseudolanuginosus*) or *Thymus praecox* 'Doretta Klaber.'

And herbs, of course. But in addition to these, one large group of annuals with perfumed leaves are the scented geraniums (*Pelargonium* hybrids). From apple to rose, pineapple, ginger and beyond, there are many *Pelargonium* varieties that are pleasing in appearance and aroma.

Garden designers often talk about designing landscapes with "a sense of place," and although they are usually speaking about the visual appearance of a garden, this phrasing could, literally, be describing aroma as well. While they may not provide the wake-up-and-smell-the-fragrance scents that many flowers produce, odors from needles and leaves are one of the sensory components that can be unique to each region.

For me, the smell of pine reminds me of childhood summers spent in canyons of the Rocky Mountains above Colorado Springs. Eucalyptus recalls the many wonderful times I've spent in northern California, and wintergreen (*Gaultheria procumbens*) brings back my junior-high ramblings in the parks and woodlands of Stevens Point, Wisconsin. Most of us have had the experience of a fragrance instantly conveying us to other times and places; it's often the closest we come to teleportation. "Beam me up, Scotty!"

If the scents of foliage take you back to pleasant times in your past, and those plants are appropriate for your garden, consider planting groups of these varieties in the landscape. Know that when it comes to foliage, the greater the number of plants placed in the garden, the more likely you are to smell their scent.

Fragrance we can do without – plants that stink

We think of fragrance as being something desirable in the garden, but there are some smells we would rather not inhale, whether they're growing naturally or not. Consider the stinkhorns, a group of fungi that appear suddenly and seemingly out of nowhere in the landscape. These are varied in appearance, but all of them are fruiting bodies, or mushrooms, that produce foul smelling odors. Think rotten meat or, yes, even dead bodies.

In addition to the dreadful smell, stinkhorns are often shocking in appearance as well. Some are phallus shaped, while others look like lobster claws or some post-Chernobyl sea creature running amuck on land. If they weren't so small, they'd be nightmare material for sure. Although these members of the *Clathraceae* and *Phallaceae* families aren't usually large, the odor they produce is formidable. Fortunately, these fungi are smelly but not harmful, and they aren't long lasting.

Stinkhorns have good reason to be so stinky. The rotting meat smell they emit attracts flies, beetles and other insects that crawl over the fruiting body, collecting spores as they do so. After walking on the fungus, and sometimes eating the smelly slime, the insects move on to other territories, spreading stinkhorn spores where they travel. It's an ingenious, if odoriferous, method of reproduction, don't you think?

If a stinkhorn arrives uninvited at your cocktail hour, you can evict this party crasher with a rake or shovel. But consider this: sometimes it's those, "You won't believe what I saw last night on the Fornaris' patio…" occasions that stay with you long after the pleasant memories fade.

Although they are only around for a couple of days, a stinkhorn fungus can provide stories to "dine out on" for years.

Stinkhorn mushrooms are impressive and interesting but not the type of cocktail hour guests that are welcome at the party. There are many types of stinkhorns, and most appear in the garden quite suddenly. They are often rudely attired in a smelly slime and usually come with an entourage of flies and beetles, which is how the spores get spread from one place to another. Other than their "something died here" odor, they are quite harmless.

A Recipe For Fragrant Success

- Scent is very subjective. If possible, always try to experience a plant's fragrance for yourself before planting it in the garden. The perfume that one person thinks is heavenly, another might perceive as overpowering. Design to please yourself, of course, but if you're planning a garden where you're likely to entertain, you might want to keep the plants with the strongest scents at a distance.

- Like any other aspect of a plant, the fragrance will be stronger when the plant is robust and happy in its location. A plant that's well-matched to its environment will produce more foliage and flowers, which will provide more sweet scents.

- If you especially love the fragrance of a particular flower or the foliage of a specific plant, use more of it in your garden. When space is an issue, grow several favored plants in containers. Even perennials and vines can be grown in large pots if you don't have enough room in the ground. In colder climates, be sure to choose a large container that won't crack over the winter.

- For scented plants that do double duty, plant them near the windows of your house. The fragrance that perfumes your cocktail hour garden will also drift into and throughout your home.

If you can't grow citrus trees in the ground, consider planting a Meyer lemon (Citrus × meyeri) in a pot. In the summer when the plant is outside, it will perfume your green hour garden all evening, and the delightfully fragrant lemons can be harvested a few months later. These citrus trees often will be in flower as the fruit matures, and they tolerate being indoors for the winter in cold climates.

You are invited

TO:

An Illuminating Encounter

WHERE:

In Your Yard & Garden

WHEN:

5 to 8 P.M.

RSVP:

To Setting Sun Plants

Three

Illumination

During the cocktail hour, nature provides just the sort of party lighting every host and hostess covets. Streams of golden rays streak across the landscape from low in the sky, giving warm backlighting to everything those slanting beams encounter. Fortunate is the homeowner whose property has a place that is lit by the sinking sun. If this describes an area in your landscape, strongly consider placing your cocktail hour garden in that illuminated location.

Illumination is one of those wonderful words that have more than one definition and a few implied meanings. Understanding how several of these apply to the cocktail hour garden can enrich the look of our landscapes and our appreciation of this evening ritual. Evening light is a magical layer of sensory experience that creates visual drama and even intellectual clarity.

This garden serves as inspiration for a cocktail hour garden that is surrounded by a slope. The variety of textures used here not only are pleasing in the late-day sun, but the use of blue foliage to contrast and cool the entire composition down is also worth noticing.

Although this border at Domaine Joly-de Lotbinière in Quebec City, Canada, wasn't planted as a cocktail hour garden, it beautifully shows how fine foliage, grasses and white flowers glow when lit from behind.

The Act of Illuminating

Illumination can be defined as the act of illuminating, or the ability of light to make something bright. The setting sun, coming at the low angle that it does, backlights plants in a way that makes the edges of flowers and foliage glow. Garden photographers often take their most arresting photographs at sunrise or sunset for this very reason. It's no wonder they call these periods "the golden hours."

Light is especially warm-toned at these times of day. In the early morning and as the sun sets, the longer, warmer wavelengths of light (the reds, oranges and yellows) are more visible to our eyes than the shorter blue light, which is more visible during the day. While these warmer wavelengths are there both in early morning and evening, during the cocktail hour it is the reds and oranges that predominate. This happens because the atmosphere has been filled with more particulate matter during the course of the day's activities, so there is more fine debris for the setting sun to shine through, making the very longest rays of the spectrum most visible.

Knowing this, the wise gardener uses a selection of plants that will be most accentuated when backlit by these warm rays in the evening. Since foliage is usually more abundant than flowers on any plant, look first to the color and texture of the leaves and stems when planning for evening illumination.

Plants that have very fine foliage are usually stunning when backlit by the late day sun. There are several plants with slender or delicate leaves that light up when the evening sun strikes them. Look for varieties with thin, small stems and foliage, and leaves that are normally lighter in color. Grasses are an excellent example of a slender, thin-leafed plant that becomes illuminated in the evening. Most grasses will catch light in this manner, but those that are yellow, red or variegated are especially beautiful during the cocktail hour.

In fact, any plant with red, orange or yellow leaves will glow in the evening light. You wouldn't want every plant in your garden to have warm-hued foliage because that wouldn't provide the contrast that makes for an interesting garden at other times of the day. But the selective placement of a yellow-leafed tree here, a red grass there, and a shrub with orange leaves or flowers there will be the equivalent of placing colored spotlights on the party decorations.

Look for plants that have thinner foliage in addition to red, yellow or variegated leaves. *Sedum* 'Metrona' has red stems and foliage, for example, but it's so thick that the sun won't illuminate this growth in the same way that it would a thinner-leafed plant.

When designing a garden, we may not think about leaving openings so that the setting sun can light up flowers and foliage. Yet, if you're lucky enough to have a property that gets evening sunshine, be sure not to plant large-growing shrubs or trees that will block that lovely light.

Plants That are Made for the Spotlight

The six plants in this first group have foliage that is fine in texture or thin enough in size so as to be translucent in the right lighting.

'MORNING LIGHT' MAIDEN GRASS
(Miscanthus sinensis 'Morning Light')
Zones 5-9

There are many varieties of maiden grass that you could invite to your cocktail hour gathering, but whether they make the guest list or not will depend on where you live, how much room you have and which variety you're thinking of planting. In many areas, the straight species, *Miscanthus sinensis*, has been declared invasive, or potentially so. Clearly, we don't want to invite a plant that will proceed to dominate the party and go on to rampage through the neighborhood! But the variety 'Morning Light' flowers late in the year, so it seldom sets seeds and is less likely to cause trouble. 'Morning Light' also has thin blades, which are perfect for backlighting, and shorter, more upright habits than other types of *Miscanthus*. This is a maiden grass that deserves to be invited to your cocktail hour.

MEXICAN FEATHER GRASS (Nasella or
Stipa tenuissima) Zones 6-10

Garden designers love this plant because of its soft, light foliage. In some parts of the country, most notably California, the plant has become an invasive thug. In those regions, put alternatives such as blue grama grass (*Bouteloua gracilis* 'Blonde Ambition') or pink muhly (see below) on the guest list instead. In much of the country, *Nasella* can be used as an annual or short-lived perennial that will sway through your party in addition to catching the evening light.

PINK MUHLY GRASS (Muhlenbergia capillaris)
Zones 5-9

The species name for this grass, *capillaris*, immediately tells us why it will be a good plant for catching the rays of the setting sun. *Capillaris* means fine, or hair-like, so this perennial shines when grown in the cocktail hour spotlight. You'll see the best performance from this North American native when it's grown in full sun and well-drained garden soil.

SWITCHGRASS (Panicum virgatum) Zones 2-9

A native grass that can attend your gathering with many costumes or personalities, switchgrass is made for backlighting. At two to four feet, its height is right, and it doesn't complain if the venue's soil is less than ideal. You have to love a plant that's willing to party even when the celebration gets completely out of hand and the grass burns to the ground! Since switchgrass evolved in prairies that were burned periodically, a few flames don't bother it at all, not that it's advisable to let your landscape burn. Be sure to leave this party guest long after the other invitees have left for the winter, since *Panicum* seeds sustain a wide range of wildlife through the cold season.

It's a common myth that King Tut papyrus (*Cyperus papyrus*) needs wet soils to thrive, but this plant proves that isn't necessarily true. Here, the papyrus thrives with *Gomphrena* 'Fireworks' and a tall marigold called Frances Hoffman's Choice, all in a garden that was deeply watered just once a week.

CALAMINT (*Calamintha nepetoides*)
Zones 5-9

This plant is always on my garden party list because it's easy, long-flowering and a pollinator magnet. Those qualities aside, it's also valuable for the cocktail hour garden because the pale, fine foliage and tiny lavender-white flowers glow when hit by the evening sun. I'm always astounded that more people don't know and grow this perennial. Invite it to your garden gathering and you won't be sorry.

KING TUT® PAPYRUS (*Cyperus papyrus*)
Zones 9-10

Most gardeners need to grow this Egyptian papyrus as an annual, and it's absolutely worth planting every year. If you're placing King Tut in a container, however, make sure it's a large and heavy pot. This papyrus grows four to six feet tall in one summer, and the explosion of hair-like, inflorescent rays on top of tall stems is dramatic, light-capturing and wind-catching. In other words, this plant brings what every party needs: drama, illumination and dance.

The following five plants will light up the cocktail hour with shades of orange and red. I advise all of you "I only plant blues, pinks and purples" people who are tempted to skip over these plants not to cheat yourself out of a colorful visual experience. Force yourself to go bold, even if it's only in a container or two.

CANNA *(Canna* hybrids*)* Zones 7-12

Although people frequently call this plant a canna lily, that's gilding the canna unnecessarily. This tropical plant is related to the banana, not the lily, and the cultivars with colorful leaves make perfect sunset catchers for containers and gardens. Look for varieties with red- or yellow-striped foliage...the brilliantly colored flowers are icing on the cake.

JAPANESE MAPLES *(Acer palmatum* or *A. japonicum* cultivars*)* Zones 5-8

You can find a red leaf maple that will mingle well in most garden parties, since there is a wide range of sizes and shapes to choose from. Look for those cultivars whose mature growth will fit in your garden. Some maples that have red foliage in the spring and fall turn green during the summer, so if you want a tree that's well attired for backlighting, look for varieties whose leaves stay colorful all season.

PURPLE SMOKE BUSH *(Cotinus coggygria* cultivars*)* Zones 4-8

The red and purple leaf varieties of *Cotinus* will have you rethinking the "No Smoking" policy at your party venue. Not that this shrub actually lights up, of course, but the hairy inflorescence that persists after the tiny flowers fade creates the illusion of smoke.

One of the top plants for green hour illumination has to be the variegated leaf canna. The large leaves cast wonderful shadows, and it's a plant that's easily grown as an annual in gardens or containers.

And because the leaves are thin, they will also glow when backlit in the evenings. Some people let their smoke bush grow large, while others chop theirs back hard every spring to stimulate new, colorful growth. Either way, this is a plant that glows at sunset.

When there are large trees on a property's perimeter, there might still be gaps where the setting sun can shine through. The rays of light through these spaces will change as the sun shifts during the course of the seasons, so make note of where they land in the months when you're most apt to be in your green hour garden and place red or golden foliage plants in those locations.

PURPLE FOUNTAIN GRASS *(Pennisetum setaceum 'Rubrum')* Zones 9-10

Those of us who garden in colder areas must be content to invite this grass to our celebrations by planting it every summer, since it's only winter hardy in limited regions. Never mind that its appearance at your party will be brief... this grass is colorful and graceful, whether it's in containers or in the garden. Other *Pennisetum* varieties that are wonderful for the cocktail hour garden include 'Fireworks,' which is variegated and a bit brighter in color, and 'Princess Caroline' or Vertigo®, large plants that don't produce flowers.

COLEUS CULTIVARS *(Plectranthus scutellarioides* or *Solenostemon scutellarioide)* Zones 10-12

With two botanical names that are both a mouthful, it's no wonder that most people continue to call this plant Coleus. No matter what name you put on these colorful plants, however, know that the newer, cutting-propagated varieties aren't the same as the Coleus your mother might have grown. Most newer varieties will thrive in sun or shade, and they don't come into bloom until very late in the fall. This means no pinching of flowers and great versatility for planting. Look for 'Red Head', 'Sedona' and the yellow-leafed 'Wasabi'; they will light up cocktail hour gardens, containers and conversations.

When the sun is sinking, yellow-foliage plants seem to absorb and then radiate those late day beams.

Yellow and white! A classy color combination in the garden at any time, but especially appreciated in the evening hours. Chardonnay Pearls *Deutzia* is a dwarf shrub that brings a lot to the party, from its bright yellow foliage to its fragrant flowers and free branching but compact shape.

FULL MOON MAPLE (*Acer shirasawanum* 'Aureum') Zones 5-7

Although there are several lovely maples that have golden foliage, this one should get a green hour invitation for its name alone. Everyone wants a full moon to rise as they relax in the garden during the evening, and if we can't always have the heavenly body itself, a plant might be a good substitute.

CHARDONNAY PEARLS® DEUTZIA (*Deutzia gracilis* 'Duncan') Zone 5-8

If there isn't much room in your cocktail hour garden, but you'd still like to invite a yellow-foliaged shrub to the gathering, look no further than this *Deutzia*. The warm-hued leaves catch the sun, and in early summer, it wears pearls to the party. This is a guest that you don't have to fuss over...it will mingle well with others and doesn't require much attention, but the color, shape and ease of this shrub will always draw your admiration.

GOLDEN PINEAPPLE SAGE (*Salvia elegans* 'Golden Delicious') Zones 8-10

Whether you grow this as an annual in colder climates or a perennial in warmer areas, golden sage arrives ready to P-A-R-T-Y. The bright yellow leaves (and I'm talking put-your-sunglasses-on brilliance) are there all summer long. As the season ends, this plant gets even more gussied up by putting on bright, lipstick-red flowers. If this isn't enough, know that *Salvia elegans* always wears her signature scent of pineapple.

HAKON GRASS (*Hakonechloa macra* 'Aureola' or 'All Gold') Zones 4-9

If I could only have one grass in my life (only one? a nightmare thought), it would be this hakon grass. Graceful, colorful and weed-smothering, *Hakonechloa macra* is equally at home in a container as it is in the perennial garden or foundation planting. 'Aureola' and 'All Gold' are must-lure-into-your-cocktail-hour plants, especially if you can provide a half-day of sun to ensure that their party attire stays its most dazzling.

Variegated plants add excitement to the garden day and night. They brighten shady areas, contrast with solid green foliage and will become illuminated if hit by the day's final sunbeams.

'ASCOT RAINBOW' SPURGE (*Euphorbia* x *martini* 'Ascot Rainbow') Zones 5-9

When the colorfully attired 'Ascot Rainbow' walks into the party, people will turn and ask, "Who is that?" The flamboyant, thin leaves are whirled around stems like festive decorations, even when they aren't lit by the setting sun. This perennial may be short lived in colder areas, but even if it just breezes through your green hour for a season or two, it's so distinctive that it's worth growing.

'COLOR GUARD' YUCCA (*Yucca filamentosa* 'Color Guard') Zones 4-10

Some guests are a bit prickly and sharp, but this contrast, especially if everyone else is being sweet and accommodating, can be quite refreshing. Since they're never actually mean, and they brighten any gathering, we welcome this aspect of their personalities. We also appreciate when such plants are deer resistant, drought tolerant and sport flowers that attract hummingbirds. So imagine my surprise when I was told that if you live in Brewster, MA, and hate your neighbor, you give them a yucca. Different strokes for different folks, I guess. Yucca 'Color Guard' is always welcome at my garden parties.

VARIEGATED JACOB'S LADDER (*Polemonium reptans* 'Stairway to Heaven') Zones 3-9

When a variegated plant has blue flowers and fine, light-catching foliage, it's destined to be invited to all the best celebrations. And when that perennial thrives in shade as well, it will immediately go on most gardeners' BFF list. Be aware that if the party gets hot, this *Polemonium* changes into all green foliage.

The variegated foliage of 'Stairway to Heaven' steals the show during early summer gatherings. Because the texture is so fine, this plant is perfect with other shade selections that have large leaves.

Just For Fun...

Sipping Sunsets

Sunset Punch

(Non-alcoholic version: substitute cranberry- or grapefruit-flavored sparkling water for the rosé)

1 tablespoon agave nectar
2 cups fresh squeezed orange juice
3 cups cold sparkling rosé
Juice of 1 lime
Sprigs of lemon verbena for garnish

Mix in a punch bowl; add ice cubes and three large sprigs lemon verbena. Garnish each glass with a sprig of lemon verbena when served.

Citrus Sunset Cocktail

(Non-alcoholic version: substitute unsweetened coconut water for the vodka and rum, along with a teaspoon of maple syrup.)

4 tablespoons blood orange juice
2 tablespoons vodka
1 tablespoon rum
4 tablespoons pineapple juice
1 slice of lime for garnish

Pour the blood orange juice into a tall glass. Add ice cubes. Mix the vodka, rum and pineapple juice and pour into the glass. Garnish with a slice of lime.

Malibu Sunset Cocktail

(Non-alcoholic version: substitute coconut milk for rum)

2 tablespoons coconut rum
1/3 cup pineapple juice
1/3 cup orange juice
Splash of cranberry juice

Linda Despres clearly knew the power that yellow foliage has when she planted this garden that rings the patio. Everyone can take inspiration from the masterful way that she combined different sizes, colors and foliage textures in this garden.

Useable Light

The second definition of illumination is the amount or strength of light that's available in a given location or for a specific purpose. For the purpose of planning a cocktail hour garden, this meaning reminds us to evaluate our spaces over time to see where brighter plants or additional lighting might be needed.

Just as yellow and variegated foliage light up when backlit by the evening sun, they also provide the illusion of illumination in darker gardens. Even if you've already placed such varieties where the sun will hit them, use more of these plants in the shady spots as well. Repeating plants with a similar foliage color at least three times in a garden unifies the design so that the plants mingle well. Think of this as checking your guest list to be sure that there are people who are either familiar with each other or who have similar tastes or experiences. A caring host wants to have good chemistry between those who are invited to the party.

Knowing where the natural light is most available also ensures that you can think about using artificial lighting where you'll get the most bang for your buck. If the setting sun is striking one part of the garden, it might not make sense to place additional lighting there. But knowing that one corner is darkest, even early in the evening, you can think about adding electric lights, candles or other methods of illumination in that dim location.

Clarification

Illumination can also refer to the process of making something easier to understand. It's this aspect of the ritual of sitting in a cocktail hour garden that's especially appealing, since it takes us out of ourselves and into the natural world. Taking time to sit and watch what's going on around us enhances our awareness of the beautiful complexity of the world we live in.

We become so used to the broad range of human busyness and business that it's often tempting to believe that there isn't much going on in our own backyards. But the richness there, on levels seen and unseen, is amazing. During a quiet time of garden observation, you might learn that fireflies aren't just blinking on and off, on and off, as the males seek to attract a mate. Each species of these beetles has its own flashing pattern, and one type of firefly even synchronizes their blinking.

You might discover that dragonflies are not only able to hover in one place, but can fly straight up or directly down as well. Perhaps you'll notice hummingbirds do indeed take time to rest, perching on nearby branches in between their foraging routes through your flowers. Or maybe you'll be fortunate enough to watch a frog eating something improbably large, such as one of the periodic cicada. If you're extremely lucky, you might be able to watch a spider construct its spiral web.

It was while sitting on my back deck, observing the garden one evening during the cocktail hour, that I discovered what was cutting the heads off my tulips and why. It was a very warm evening for late spring, and I decided to indulge in what is normally a summer ritual and sit out on the deck in the early evening. I sat and watched the setting sun light up random shrubs and trees and appreciated when a thin ray hit the flowerbeds that were planted in the terraced hillside.

Most of the perennials were just beginning to emerge in this terraced area, but scattered in and among them were some red and coral tulips that I'd planted the previous fall. I loved the fact that this small sunbeam hit four or five of these tulips, as if a lighting engineer had trained his spotlights onto a stage. Other than this unexpected tulip illumination, it initially seemed like nothing much was happening in this spring landscape.

After a few minutes, however, the wildlife that had skittered away to hide when I arrived began to resume their evening routines. Chickadees flew in to perch first on the branches of a *Viburnum*, pausing just seconds to be sure the coast was clear before flying to the birdfeeder to grab a seed. The goldfinches and nuthatches soon followed, taking turns in what seemed like a well-choreographed dance that combined self-interest and cooperation.

I watched as a gray squirrel emerged from the property line and hopped under the birdfeeder. It rummaged in the grass around the pole for a few minutes, picking up seeds that the birds had kicked off of the dish above. After a few minutes, the squirrel left the feeder and jumped to the top of the first terrace wall. It hopped into the flowerbed, and I briefly thought that perhaps this squirrel was going to bury some birdseed there. Maybe there will be sunflowers growing in this garden next summer, I thought, and I'll know just who planted them.

The gray squirrel didn't have seed sowing on his mind, however. As I sat very still, I saw him move directly to one of the coral tulips, rise up on his back legs so that his head was even with the flower, and with his front paws and mouth bite the tulip blossom right off, letting it fall to the ground. I was so surprised that at first I didn't react. When I saw what happened next, I was glad that I didn't immediately leap to my feet to scold him, because what I observed was as illuminating as the sunbeam this critter was perched in.

After the tulip flower fell to the ground, the squirrel stayed by the stalk, still up on his hind feet. I watched

as he paused there for a few seconds, and then began to lick the top of the recently severed stem. As the plant continued to bring liquid up the tulip stalk, that squirrel was using it as his own personal drinking fountain! It was his own cocktail hour garden moment.

Of course I wasn't thrilled that this critter had decapitated my tulips, nor that he, or another squirrel, continued to do so until I sprinkled them all with cayenne pepper. But it was good to know why the tulips were being attacked. Had I not just sat and watched, I never would have known why an animal would commit this seemingly pointless act of vandalism.

A setting sun doesn't just illuminate the plants in a cocktail hour garden, but can create shadow patterns that are magical in the evening. When designing your green hour environment, it can be fun to place assorted potted plants along the edge of a patio or walkway and see which casts the most interesting shadows.

Enlightenment

The fourth definition of illumination that might apply to a cocktail hour garden is an arrival of intellectual or spiritual insight. Although this is related to clarification and comes from the same willingness to be still for a period of time, the illumination in this case does not come from watching the external world. Mystical, inspirational or cerebral illumination arises from that complex place inside, where what is in the mind suddenly connects with something mysterious and non-physical.

Sudden bursts of creativity, inspiration or new levels of understanding seem to happen most frequently when people step out of their day-to-day business and allow their spirit and mind some breathing room. There are many stories of ideas, perceptions and inventions that are suddenly clear to people as they stand on the beach or are walking without a definite destination. Many companies, knowing the value of giving their employees time to play without purpose, encourage the staff to take regular periods to let thoughts and creations bubble to the surface.

The cocktail hour garden is the perfect environment for the cultivation of enlightenment. You are invited to come for the light show, enjoy the entertainment and leave enriched.

Party Planning:
A Recipe for Illuminating Success

- When planning plantings that will be backlit, get several thin bamboo poles of various lengths and tie some white, yellow or red ribbons near their tops. Sit in your garden at sunset and look at the places where the light shines and place one of the bamboo stakes there. Notice where the ribbons are backlit and show up well and on which size stakes these ribbons are tied. This will help you to plan which plants will be best placed in those locations.

- For successful back lighting, the plants chosen should have some parts that are thin enough for the sun to shine though. These could be leaves, of course, but the foliage isn't the only part of the plant that can be translucent. Flowers, seeds and even thorns can all be made luminous when the sun hits them.

- In addition to noting which locations the sun illuminates, spend several evenings watching where shadows fall in the landscape. These areas can be brightened with plants that have white and green variegated foliage or those that have white flowers.

- All good garden design depends on balancing a variety of colors and textures of foliage. So even in those areas where the sun shines late in the day, include some plants that are not going to be backlit. You'll appreciate those with fine textures, red or yellow colors or variegated leaves much more if they are offset by leaves that are larger and some that are dark green.

You are invited

TO:

A Landscape that Glows

WHERE:

In Your Yard & Garden

WHEN:

5 to 8 P.M.

RSVP:

To White and Silver

Four

Sunset: After-Twilight Plants and Lighting

*I*n mid-summer the green hours are well illuminated by the long-day sun, but at other times our cocktail gatherings may be wrapped in darkness. Instead of a cause for despair, however, the blackness of night is an opportunity for creating garden drama, romantic lighting or cozier gathering places.

Full darkness provides a whole new perspective on the landscape. As surrounding trees lose their color and become black shapes against the sky, we can see their forms without being distracted by the colors and details of the foliage. It's easier to appreciate that some trees have vase-like profiles, while others are rounded and spreading. Trees such as black tupelo or some swamp maples have branches that shoot around helter-skelter, frequently at odd angles. Pine and palm trees show off their classic silhouettes and all are seen differently as the sky darkens.

Gardens change too, as evening moves into night, with some plants becoming more prominent while others disappear completely. So, the design of a cocktail hour garden usually includes plants that are visible even as night falls. Along with plant varieties that are more noticeable in the dark, many people also like to use lighting as another way to set particular moods in the landscape. The judicious or playful use of artificial lighting can produce a dramatic scene, create a party atmosphere or fashion a romantic ambiance. All of this would not be possible in the daylight hours.

Silver and White

Plants that come dressed in silver or white are perfect for the cocktail hour garden. Even without additional lighting, these plants are visible and attractive in beds and containers. When designing a garden for the green hour, you can't go wrong with white flowers and silver foliage.

Additionally, silver-foliaged plants are functional for other reasons. These stylish silvers are useful for lining pathways through the garden or to and from seating areas, providing markers that will guide people even in the absence of lighting. Gray foliage plants are often more drought and heat tolerant, because the fine white hairs that cover the foliage help reflect the sun and retain water. Finally, many silver plants won't be nibbled by the rabbits and deer that stroll through your cocktail-hour gatherings.

In most areas, dusty miller *(Senecio cineraria)* is commonly sold in six-packs as an annual. That makes it affordable to mix many plants with additional annuals, so that the silver foliage weaves in and among other colors. In this combination of *Salvia* 'Vista Red and White' and Persian shield *(Strobilanthes dyeranus)*, the white in the *Salvia* blooms and the silver tops of the Persian shield leaves help unite the entire planting.

Plants With Silver Foliage

Here are a few stylish silvers that will shine in your gardens day and night.

WORMWOOD *(Artemisia 'Powis Castle')*
Zones 6-10 and *(A. schmidtiana 'Silver Mound')*
Zones 4-9

Some *Artemisia* species wander around the party, inserting themselves into every conversation in the garden and generally making a pest of themselves. Don't confuse 'Powis Castle' and 'Silver Mound' with those drifters. These two wormwoods are the better-behaved, clump forms of this popular silver plant. The worst that you can say about 'Silver Mound' is that flowering makes the plant a bit floppy and sloppy, so when it starts to splay open while it blooms, cut it right to the ground. It will soon be back and on its best behavior.

JAPANESE PAINTED FERN
(Athyrium niponicum hybrids) Zones 4-9

There are many wonderful varieties of this colorful shade plant, and they wear colorful clothing and makeup that's perfect for your festivities. In addition to silver frosting on the leaves, many arrive with red stems and shades of purple, blue and green on the foliage. Anyone looking for more color in a shade garden can't go wrong with these ferns. Just be sure to cluster them together...for this perennial, more is more.

If ever there was a plant designed for moonlight, it is this *Artemisia*. Like many in this genus, 'Valerie Finnis' (May we call you Valerie?) spreads, but she is far more restrained than her rambunctious cousins, 'Silver King' and 'Silver Queen', who clearly feel entitled as royalty to take over your garden kingdom. Send Valerie an invitation to your evening garden but leave the royals off the guest list.

Silver foliage calls attention to itself, so it can be tricky to place it so that it's well blended into the garden instead of standing out as light gray dots in a green background. One way of working silvers in effectively is to place them near other plants that are equally attention getting, such as these lilies. Another trick is to use plants that have a very fine texture, such as this *Artemisia* 'Parfum d'Ethiopia'.

HEARTLEAF BUGLOSS *(Brunnera macrophylla* 'Jack Frost'*)* Zones 3-8

Another silver-bedecked perennial for shade, every spring 'Jack Frost' arrives sprinkled with blue flowers that are similar to forget-me-nots. This agreeable plant was selected as the 2012 Perennial Plant of the Year, which is the Perennial Plant Association's equivalent of Most Likely to Succeed. It is sure to illuminate shady garden parties long after the cocktail hour graduates into night.

CARDOON *(Cynara cardunculus)* Zones 7-9

In climates that are hotter or colder than its narrow range for hardiness, cardoon can be invited to your green hour as an annual. While it's true that in some parts of California this plant has escaped from the party and become a weed, elsewhere this Mediterranean native is appreciated for its prickly, sharp, silver foliage. In many parts of the world, cardoon is welcomed for its artichoke-flavored stalks, but in the United States we tend to focus on the thistle-like flowers and foliage. Even though it's edible, don't look to this plant to step in should the snacks at your cocktail hour run out. In order to make the stalks tender, the leaves have to be bound around the stems with wrapping for up to six weeks.

SILVER NICKEL VINE (*Dicondra argentea* 'Silver Falls') Zones 10-12

If the Tin Man from The Wizard of Oz and Rapunzel had children, I imagine their offspring would have long, metallic hair just like *Dicondra* 'Silver Falls.' Silver nickel vine is very adaptable and happy to grow quickly as an annual in cold climates or as a perennial ground cover where it's warm.

DUSTY MILLER (*Jacobaea maritima* aka *Senecio cineraria*) Zones 8-10

Dusty miller has been a favorite at garden parties in all areas of the country for years, often arriving in a crowd as six-pack annuals. Although the plant is listed as only being cold hardy to Zone 8, many gardeners in colder areas find that the *Jacobaea maritima* plants in their flowerbeds or containers live through the winter. Since dusty miller doesn't spread out too wide, gardeners are advised to group several plants together in order to avoid a polka-dot look.

LICORICE PLANT (*Helichrysum petiolare* 'White Licorice') Zones 10-11

To most gardeners in the country, this trailing annual is an explosive party guest. When it arrives, the round, silver leaves seem so sweet and delicate that many people don't realize that, in a container, only one of these plants is needed. Given some root room, fertilizer and warm weather, 'White Licorice' becomes white lightning, sprawling through, around and up neighboring plants. Owing to its tendency to ramble, licorice plant makes a good weaver and knitter, unifying beds or large pots or providing a fast annual ground cover. Where this *Helichrysum* is hardy, it is usually treated as a shrub.

BLUE SWITCH GRASS (*Panicum amarum* 'Dewey Blue') Zones 2-9

It's nice to have a grass that doesn't seem to care if the party venue is cold, hot, dry or humid. A native plant from the coast of Delaware, 'Dewey Blue' is useful as a single specimen or when planted in drifts. Think of this plant for covering a difficult sunny slope as well. Although it can get 4 to 5 feet tall, switch grass is willing to pitch in as a soil-stabilizing ground-cover that maintains its good looks through the fall and winter.

LUNGWORT (*Pulmonaria* 'Silver Bouquet' and 'Silver Shimmers') Zone 3-8

Don't you think that an elegant shade plant with silver foliage and sweet spring flowers deserves a better common name than lungwort? Never mind that wort derives from the old English word *wyrt*, which meant plant, and the German *wurtiz*, meaning root. And yes, wort often signifies that a plant was used medicinally, so clearly it was once thought that *Pulmonaria* had some value for the lungs. Neverthe-less, when introducing these to others at your green hour gatherings, perhaps it's best just to say, "And have you met *Pulmonaria* 'Silver Bouquet'?"

Did You Know...
About Crepuscular Creatures?

Animals and insects that are active at night are said to be nocturnal, and those that operate during the day are called diurnal. But there is a sizeable group of beings that come to life only in the hours in between day and night. Unfortunately, these creatures that are active during the cocktail hour aren't called cocktailturnal.

From tiny insects to larger birds, reptiles or mammals, these are known as crepuscular creatures. Crepuscular is defined as "occurring or active during twilight" or "relating to or resembling twilight." Such wildlife hides out during the day and sleeps at night. Within the crepuscular group there are two subcategories of animals, because some critters become lively in the evening hours (vespertine) while others (matutinal) are active only around dawn. Finally, a third group mixes it up between twilight and early morning.

For some animals, this arrangement evolved as a means of avoiding predators, since those hunters looking for prey in the day or night have a harder time seeing in twilight hours. Others may have developed this pattern as a way to conserve resources by avoiding hot days or cold nights.

Crepuscular mammals include hamsters, rabbits, otters and possums. Two reptiles in this category are rattlesnakes and gila monsters. There are many insects that are crepuscular, including several moths, beetles and our particular nemesis: many types of mosquitos.

Did You Know...
About the Second Shift at the Plant Food Factory?

During the day plants are photosynthesizing, using sunlight to convert carbon dioxide and water into carbohydrates. The day shift, with the presence of sunlight, both creates energy and burns or stores what has been produced. During the evening cocktail hour, however, they switch from this production *and* consumption mode to usage and storage methods.

At night, the plant burns much, but not all, of the starches that were produced during the day. They use that energy primarily for their growth. How do plants know how much of those carbohydrates to burn? And what happens if the day is shorter so they can't put as much starch into storage?

Research shows that plants have a mechanism for figuring out the amount of carbohydrates they can use at night based on the length of light during the day. In other words, they are on a 24-hour clock and able to quickly adjust how much starch they burn to the hours of photosynthesizing they were able to do. If the days are longer and they produce more carbohydrates, they burn a larger percentage and at a faster rate. But if the days are shorter and they aren't stockpiling as much energy, they burn less and they use the energy at a slower rate.

The Moon Garden

For centuries, it's been fashionable to design gardens that are visible by the light of the moon. From The Moonlight Garden planted at the Taj Mahal in the 1500s to the moonbeam-themed gardens of the Victorian era, plantings designed for night viewing have continued to fascinate.

As with a theme garden, social gatherings too have long been planned around an idea or subject matter.

From masked balls to costume parties, organizing a celebration around special clothing has appealed to many who are planning festivities. A recent tradition is the white party, a gathering where all the guests are requested to wear white.

Whether your cocktail hour has a dress code or is come-as-you-are, here are some white flowering plants that will stand out after dark.

It's no wonder this plant prefers its common name, whirling butterflies, to the botanical label *Gaura lindheimeri*. The scientific name is great for accuracy, of course, but in the cocktail hour garden romance trumps precision every time. Delicate white flowers that sway in the breeze and are visible as the light fades are the reason that this plant is on the guest list, even in places where it's an annual.

DAPPLED WILLOW (Salix integra 'Hakuro Nishiki') Zones 4-9

Thin, graceful and willing to grow as a shrub or small tree, the dappled willow fits into many landscapes and manages to be showy and subtle at the same time. "How does she *do* it?" the other guests murmur enviously. Since the tree form of 'Hakuro Nishiki' is grafted onto another willow's trunk, it never grows too high, the leaves are thin and the new growth has just the right amount of pink along with the green and white. 'Hakuro Nishiki' can even be grown in a pot, but if you're planning to leave it outside in the winter, you should have a large, unbreakable container and be in a warm Zone 6 or above. All that aside, this is a graceful tree that not only shows up well as the sky darkens but is the perfect plant to illuminate with some dramatic up-lighting. Like most *Salix*, this plant is thirsty, so don't wait too long before you offer it a drink.

DIAMOND FROST® EUPHORBIA (Euphorbia hypericifolia 'Inneuphdia') Zones 10-11

'Diamond Frost' is a versatile annual in most parts of the country; it looks good when several plants are placed together in annual or perennial beds, and it plays well with others in pots and boxes. My friend Andy Aiken used to say that this plant was his "secret weapon" in containers. He meant that he could put one in any mixed annual box or pot and it made the entire composition look better – the tiny white flowers almost star-like, seeming to twinkle as the green hour fades into night.

GIANT FLEECE FLOWER (Persicaria polymorpha) Zones 3-8B

Only invite this perennial to your cocktail hour garden if you're willing to give it plenty of space – lots and *lots* of space. This is the party guest that starts out looking innocent enough but over time is seen to fill a huge area in size and personality. Think *Astilbe* on steroids. Think rock star with big, white hair. But in addition to showy, think easy and long-flowering as well.

'BLUE RIVER II' HARDY HIBISCUS (Hibiscus moscheutos 'Blue River II') Zones 4-10

Having a 'Blue River II' hardy hibiscus in the garden is like having a plant filled with full moons every night. Although each individual white flower is only open for 24 hours, they are huge, round and as crisp-looking as freshly-starched linen. And the flowering period is at least four weeks, providing many moonrises on many nights. If you have enough space in your cocktail hour garden, this hibiscus combines well with the giant fleece flower in that their sizes are complementary, and 'Blue River II' starts flowering as the *Persicaria* blooms wind down.

PINKY WINKY® HYDRANGEA (Hydrangea paniculata 'DVPpinky') Zones 3-9

Since Pinky Winky is one of the *paniculatas*, it is bone hardy and reliable in addition to being lovely. Most *Hydrangea paniculata* varieties are perfect for shining during the cocktail hour and into the night. Some of the smaller varieties can even be used in containers.

Pinky Winky has the advantage of upright flowers that develop a pinkish (no surprise, given the name) tint as they age. It's a show business plant with a show business name.

PHLOX 'DAVID' (Phlox paniculata 'David') Zones 4-8

If your cocktail hour garden is sunny, P. 'David' should be on the guest list. He glows after dark, is sweetly scented, laughs at powdery mildew and arrives with flowers for your table arrangements and bouquets.

One of most beautiful white flowers is larger than a dinner plate. Hibiscus 'Blue River II' fills the perennial garden with round flowers that speak of full moons, starched petticoats or white parasols.

If "no-brainer" was a horticultural term, it would be used in every Phlox 'David' plant tag and catalog listing.

'STAR CLUSTER' TICKSEED (Coreopsis 'Star Cluster') Zones 5-9

We have to admit that this Coreopsis isn't really white. Not bridal gown white, anyway. If it arrived wearing these flowers at a true white party, people would admire the blossoms while complaining that perhaps 'Star Cluster' had misread the invitation. The flowers on this Coreopsis are a creamy white, and as the weather cools the centers get etched with varying shades of pink. But since this perennial blossoms for so long, and the light flowers do indeed show up after twilight, everyone at your cocktail hour gatherings will simply smile and party on.

WHITE PROFUSION ZINNIAS (Zinnia Profusion hybrid) Annuals everywhere

The Profusion series of hybrid zinnias has been an out and out gift to gardeners who want a tidy annual that flowers all summer with little to no care. They come in show-in-the-dark white as well as other colors, love the heat and bring their friends, the butterflies, along with them.

Nothing New Under the Sun...or Moon

Country Life in America was a lifestyle magazine published in the early 1900s. An article in Volume 23, March 1913, contained a reference to the moon garden. This section, from a story called "In The Dark O' The Moon" by Ida M. H. Starr, shows that planting for visibility at night has been of interest to gardeners for a long time.

"Come with me," I said to the Horticulturist, "I wish to show you my moon garden."

"Your moon garden? Lord a'mercy! What's that?"

"Oh it's a place where flowers that love the night, azure, white, silver gray, and lavender – ghost flowers – bloom; where it is always still and peaceful; where no one ever hurries; where you wait for the moon to tell you the time to do things; where all manner of powers that people ordinarily do not consider, float down from the stars to make things grow; where the gardener hears wonderful sounds stealing down from the milky way, for he has time to listen, you know; where Venus, Mars, Jupiter, Saturn, and all the planets work together to help."

Helen McVeigh and Bobby Hallstein make a good team when designing gardens that shine in the evening hours. Helen's use of white flowers throughout this garden and Bobby's woodwork and birdhouses are beautifully combined in this summer garden.

Artificial Lighting

Perhaps you've seen the T-shirts that read, "If all the world's a stage, then I want better lighting." Since designing a garden has many parallels to planning a stage set, it's only natural that lighting should be part of the plan. And just as it is in the theater, lights that enhance the cocktail-hour garden are chosen for a combination of pure function and dramatic effect.

Functional lighting includes electric lights on buildings, down paths and along stairs. Most of these lights illuminate for the purpose of seeing the area well. They may be put on dimmers in order to allow flexibility in brightness, but the main purpose of this lighting is to make spaces safe and visible.

Hardwired lighting can also be used for dramatic effect, especially when the subject of the illumination is a plant or garden ornament. Spotlights at the base of trees, fountains with lighting in their pools or outdoor bulbs hidden among rocks, pond edges or trained onto sculptures all create an atmosphere of mystery. They can make small areas appear larger by drawing the eye to the perimeters of the property, while the darkness beyond hints that there might actually be more. In large, open yards, where there actually is more space beyond the cocktail-hour garden, this lighting creates spaces that are more intimate.

Lighting selected plants from below is a wonderful way to add drama to the garden. Trees with variegated foliage, such as this dappled willow (*Salix* 'Hakuro Nishiki'), are especially well-suited for this theatrical lighting, because the white leaves are already more visible at night.

Since lighting draws insects at night, placing lights away from where people will gather makes sense practically while still setting the right mood and illuminating areas for safety. An electrician and the professionals at your local lighting supply store can help you to determine which fixtures and wiring are right for your landscape.

Stringing small lights up trees is a way to sprinkle a few stars closer to the garden.

Beyond permanent lighting, however, is the whole world of decorative illumination. Fairy lights, candles, patio string lights and paper lanterns are easy to install and fun to play with. You can change the look of your garden every weekend if you have a mind to.

FAIRY LIGHTS. Wind fairy lights (aka Christmas lights) around tree trunks or drip them from the branches. There are so many more options beyond the white or green-corded lighting from years ago. LED lights on wires that disappear are particularly useful, and they are available battery or electricity powered. These can be strung in plants, hung from the ceiling, wound into rattan or twig screening or circled up obelisks. Any glass object such as old vases, vintage ceiling lights, mason jars, wine bottles or gazing globes can be made into creative garden lighting with these small LED strings.

CANDLES. Similarly, candles, be they real or digital, can be placed throughout the garden. Metal candelabras can be placed among plants, or groups of candles can be clustered in a birdbath. Tea lights can be placed into vintage vases or other glassware and placed around the garden. Just make sure that real fire-burning wax candles are far away from mulch,

dried leaves or the areas where people walk. Always assume that any real candle will burn down before it is blown out and locate it where this can happen without being a fire hazard.

PATIO STRING LIGHTS. These are available in many styles. If you don't have a structure to hang them from, use very tall poles stuck into large, heavy flowerpots that are filled with dirt. Plant flowering plants around the poles and run the lighting from pole to pole to define your sitting area. String lights can also be hung from trees or large bushes or clustered under a large sun umbrella.

PAPER LANTERNS. For special occasions, there is nothing like paper lanterns to provide a romantic party atmosphere. Many of them are inexpensive enough to hang at the start of the summer and leave in place through the season, especially in regions that don't get driving summer rainfalls. Although paper lanterns were originally lit with real candles, most people now use the digital tea lights, electric bulbs or other battery operated flames so that they don't have to worry about the possibility of a fire.

Like string lighting, lanterns can be hung from trees, arbors or buildings. For instant drama in open spaces, place two very tall, flexible bamboo or fiberglass poles in the ground or in pots, secured in the soil and about six feet apart. Bend the poles to each other and tie them together with wire, creating an arch, and hang one or more paper lantern inside each of the arches that the poles have created. The arch frames the lantern or lanterns, as well as providing a support for the lights.

Party Planning:
A Recipe for Brighter Planting

The double-flower mock orange shrub (Philadelphus x virginalis varieties) has white blooms that are not only visible in evening light but are intoxicatingly fragrant as well.

● Don't plant too few or too many silver-foliaged plants. Too few will look dotted and pull your eye from other plantings. But too many will turn your entire garden gray, which won't be a good look in the daytime in most regions. In garden design, balance comes from repetition and contrast. Consider using three different silver-foliaged plants in a garden and make their groups roughly equivalent in size or "weight" of the leaves. In other words, a silver plant with fine foliage might be used in a larger group, but one with large, bold leaves could be planted singularly or in a smaller grouping.

● When planting flowerbeds with a white party theme, keep in mind that light petals often show fading sooner than other colors; edges that are turning brown aren't as noticeable on a dark pink flower as they are on a white one. That said, a white garden can be lovely as long as you include flowers of different sizes and shapes for contrast. If the foliage is also chosen for an assortment of colors and textures, the garden will be lovely no matter what is in bloom.

● Those who frequently use their cocktail hour garden after dark may want to consider a screened porch for insect protection. Screened rooms haven't been in vogue in recent years, as the popularity of decks and three-season rooms have risen and more people have air conditioning. But in some areas of the country, there is renewed interest in screened porches or gazebos, often outfitted with outdoor fireplaces, chandeliers and other combinations of rustic and formal styles. If a screened room is part of your green

hour gatherings, consider planting fragrant flowers outdoors around the perimeter and include greenery such as ferns or other low-light houseplants inside.

● Outdoor lighting is especially nice when the brightness is adjustable. Place your cocktail hour garden lights on dimmers whenever possible, so that the illumination can be fine-tuned according to the gathering and the desired mood.

● Have fun with it.

You are invited

~∞~

TO:

Watch Color Take Flight

WHERE:

In Your Yard & Garden

WHEN:

5 to 8 P.M.

RSVP:

To Larvae and Butterflies

Five

Planting for Butterflies

Question: How is the cocktail hour garden similar to a benefit ball?

Answer: Everyone enjoys looking at what others are wearing, while having a great time and supporting a good cause.

Having butterflies attend your cocktail hour gathering is like hosting a party where flowers are set into flight. Color, movement and grace with a dash of unpredictability...these are four qualities that are guaranteed to make a gathering come alive. It's no wonder that we want to plant flowers that attract these elegantly-attired winged creatures to our gardens. Yet in present times, the desire to have butterflies in our landscapes goes beyond a selfish desire to enjoy their beauty and moves into the realm of environmental awareness.

Agastache 'Blue Fortune' is always on my cocktail hour A-list because of the long-blooming period of its the pale lavender flowers. This plant also attracts hummingbirds and butterflies, such as this eastern tiger swallowtail.

The Good Cause

We don't all have the space for a bug field such as this one at Seaside Daylily Farm on Martha's Vineyard, but the philosophy is one we can all embrace. Nature usually keeps things in balance, and we can help by providing places where beneficial insects, predators and pollinators will thrive. Even a small yard can leave a strip of native plants (aka weeds) in the back or a side yard.

In many parts of the world, there has been a decline in the population of insects. We're most familiar, of course, with the swiftly dwindling populations of butterflies and bees, and this has prompted public awareness about the importance of what people can do in their own yards and gardens that might help. In the cocktail hour garden and beyond, most people want to support pollinators and butterflies. This requires us to be extra thoughtful about our backyards and beyond.

As human populations have grown, we have spread out into former fields and woodlands. Anyone over the age of 50 can tell you stories of how their hometown spread into what was the farmlands or wild areas of their youth. Add to that expansion our desire to tame our landscapes or "clean things up," and it's no wonder that populations of insects and animals have a hard time finding places where they can thrive as they did in the past.

This isn't a book about wildlife conservation, but when we design any garden there is an overlap between creating an environment that comforts and pleases us but also strengthens or works *with* the natural world. Here is where the definition of the green hour expands to mean "natural, pure, eco-friendly and organic." Here is another way we can explore the power we have to create change and celebrate our desire to make a difference in the world. Here is a place where we lift a glass to the way

Pamela Phipps made a deliberate decision not to have a lawn on her property. Her home is surrounded by gardens that are not only beautiful but very butterfly friendly.

everything is connected to everything else, while designing our gardens so that we can appreciate and follow nature.

There are several things that homeowners can do to assist in the return of healthy insect populations. From the plants we include to those we remove, the style of our landscapes and the way we maintain them, every action might play a role in helping to sustain wildlife. It comes down to being careful about all aspects of our yards and gardens.

Let's look at a property from a bird, bee and butterfly's point of view, beginning on the edges and moving inward to gardens designed for the green hour. To begin with, our winged creatures want to see areas of a yard that are left a bit natural in a way that creates a wildlife-sustaining buffer. Most properties can accommodate a section of the back or side yard that remains on the wild and weedy side.

As little as twenty years ago, this would be seen as sloppy or negligent, but fashions change. Today,

those in the know realize that this is a thoughtful way to protect the wildlife we're connected to. Hopefully, neighborhoods can begin to look at empty lots and fields not as eyesores but as wildlife preserves, where ground-nesting birds, bees, butterflies and more can find the shelter and food that they depend on.

Similarly, gardeners know that such areas are also home to the predators that keep everything in balance. These insects and animals are nature's way of making sure that large populations of any one genus or species don't take over the landscape. They are the ladybugs that feed on our aphids, for example, and the parasitic wasps that keep tomato hornworms in check. But in order for nature to maintain equilibrium and diversity, she depends on us to do the same.

Homeowners might choose to minimize the expanse of lawns. When Mother Nature designs a landscape, she doesn't plan for large monocultures that are regularly clipped low. She doesn't design areas to be tended with so many products that they become barren, green deserts. She realizes that stretches of turf sustain nothing but the lawn care industry.

So a wild buffer and less lawn are two things that the Three B's would like to see. They would also say that a brush pile or two, layers of foliage and a delay of fall cleanup are also important. Wildlife, including butterflies, need to have sheltering places in the winter. Most gardeners only think about attracting the actual colorful butterflies to their garden with flowers, but many of these beauties have to over-winter in cold climates. Since butterflies don't spend their entire life dressed up in their fancy party wings, we also need to remember to support the other phases of these creatures' lives. Depending on the species, they can overwinter as butterflies, pupae or caterpillars, and the average American lawn doesn't supply much protection for any of those.

Similarly, if part of an insect's life cycle is attaching a cocoon to the stem of a plant or the underside of a leaf, cutting down or disposing of that plant material in the fall would destroy that wintering place. This is not to say that we should leave all of our properties untended. But if there's a choice between cutting down perennials and grasses in the fall or in the spring, doing it after winter is over just might provide additional protection to threatened species.

In addition to winter safety, butterflies need nectar, water, warmth and mud when they're winged and food when they're in the larval stage. Warmth and mud? Yes, indeed. Butterflies can't self regulate body temperatures, so they depend on being able to find warm rocks that have absorbed the heat of the sun. They drink muddy water in order to take in the minerals they need; mud is more or less the butterfly equivalent of a nutrient drink. And remember to accept a certain level of imperfection in the garden: those *Asclepias* plants with holes and chomped leaves might have been eaten by monarch larvae. So, planting for butterflies is a matter of supporting all three forms that a butterfly takes: the winged creature, the larva and the pupae/cocoon.

A Toast To Butterflies and Bees!

Raise your glass to both of these winged beauties and our efforts to support and save them.

The Butterfly Cocktail

I understand that this cocktail was created by Alex Kammer-ling, a British writer, mixologist and author of Blend Me, Shake Me.

> 8 seedless white grapes
> 1.5 oz. vodka
> ¼ oz. elderflower liqueur
> ¼ oz. freshly squeezed lemon juice
> 3 leaves basil
> 3 leaves mint
> Ice

Muddle the grapes in a shaker, add the other ingredients and shake to blend. Strain into a chilled martini glass and garnish with a lemon twist.

The Iron Butterfly

> 1.5 oz. vodka
> 1.5 oz. coffee liqueur (Kahlua, etc.)
> 1.5 oz. Bailey's Irish Cream

Add these into a glass over ice. Optional garnish is a twist of orange peel or a chocolate covered coffee bean.

The Flutter By

Since butterflies are so delicate, it seems to me that a drink that pays homage to them would also be light and a tad elusive. This beverage can be made alcoholic or not, but either way it's very refreshing. Note that raw coconut milk is often pink, adding to this drink's appeal.

> 2 sprigs lemon verbena
> 1.5 oz. fresh squeezed orange juice
> 3 or more drops of the hot sauce of your choice (I use Outerbridge's Original Sherry Peppers Sauce)
> 4 oz. coconut water (not coconut milk)
> Edible flowers of your choice

Optional:

> 2 oz. 100% agave tequila
> Ice

Put the lemon verbena sprigs in the bottom of a tall glass and crush them a bit with a spoon. Add ice, crushed or in cubes. Pour in orange juice first, add the two drops of hot sauce and also add tequila (if desired). Pour the coconut water into the glass and garnish with fresh, edible flowers. Suggestions include petals from organically grown pansies, marigolds, roses, bee balm, lavender, tulips, peonies, nasturtiums or any of the flowers from edible herbs.

While we're toasting our attention to the butterflies, let's salute the bees as well. And what better way to celebrate than with drinks made with honey. Here are two cocktail recipes courtesy of Stephanie Krieger, owner of Nani Moon Meadery, in Kapaa, Hawaii.

Deviant Basil Mojito

Sprigs of fresh basil
½ oz. fresh lime juice
½ oz. Sambal Oelek hot sauce or
    chili pepper jelly
½ oz. simple syrup if you haven't used
    the jelly
1.5 oz. Deviant Beehavior Mead
1 oz. spiced rum
2 oz. pineapple juice
Ice
Sparkling mineral water

Muddle at least six basil leaves in a mason jar. Add lime juice, hot sauce (or pepper jelly), syrup, mead, rum and juice. Mix well and add ice cubes. Top with mineral water to fill the glass and garnish with a sprig of basil.

Winter Sun Margarita

1 oz. Winter Sun Mead
1 oz. premium tequila
½ oz. Grand Marnier
1 oz. fresh squeezed tangelo juice
½ oz. fresh lime juice
Raw honey to taste
A pinch of Hawaiian sea salt
Ice

Mix all ingredients in a shaker or mason jar with a lid and shake vigorously. Add ice cubes and garnish with an orange or tangelo slice.

Mixing Wild and Tame

Professional gardener Pamela Phipps knows that an attractive garden contains a variety of foliage shapes and sizes. In her cottage garden, the large milkweed leaves provide a nice contrast to the finer leaves, and the upright, variegated foliage makes a visually pleasing garden that is also monarch friendly.

There are several design strategies for mixing wildlife support plants and sustaining practices into your landscape. The simplest is to add butterfly plants to existing flower gardens, shrub borders and container groupings. Even such a wild child such as common milkweed (*Asclepias syriaca*) can be attractively tucked among your other perennials and grasses.

On properties that are large enough, a wildflower and grasses meadow can be planted with native perennials, and this can be screened from the rest of the landscaping with a mixed shrub border. By planting a variety of shrubs that flower at different times, the shrubs will do double duty by providing both a dividing screen between wild and tame and a foraging area for bees and birds.

We can invite butterflies to our cocktail hour with rock walls, paths or even single stones where they can perch to stay warm. Some create depressions where regular irrigation can collect even briefly in the mud puddles that these winged insects use for mineral collecting. Unfortunately, the boxes commonly sold as butterfly shelters seem to be more attractive to people than they are to the creatures they are intended for. It seems that butterflies would rather hide in brush, hollow trees or other natural crevices than in a manmade box.

Cocktail Hour Invitations for Butterflies

These plants should be on the menu if you want butterflies to attend
your green hour gatherings.

ASTERS, including 'Raydon's Favorite' (*Symphyotrichum oblongifolium* aka *Aster oblongifolius*) Zones 3-8

There are many asters that could be included on a butterfly menu, but we'll highlight 'Raydon's Favorite' as this book's "daily special," because its size works so well in sunny gardens. This variety grows between two and three feet tall and produces violet-blue flowers for three weeks or more in the fall. Perfect for the butterfly that comes late to the party!

'AUTUMN JOY' SEDUM (*Sedum* 'Herbstfreude') Zones 3-8

Sedum Autumn Joy is a cast iron plant for full sun that is favored by bees as well as butterflies. Put this on the menu if you've got a hot, dry location in full sun. Don't place this plant where it will be frequently watered or fertilized, however, as the tall *Sedums* are generally stronger and more attractive when grown in lean soils.

COREOPSIS (*Coreopsis* spp.) Zones 3-11

There are many wonderful varieties of coreopsis, and butterflies seem to love them all, so pick the colors, sizes and types according to how they will blend with the other options in your butterfly buffet. Know that a couple of varieties of coreopsis, the bright yellow 'Zagreb' and pink *C. rosea*, are better planted as groundcovers rather than flower garden elements because they just don't play well with others.

BUTTERFLY BUSH (*Buddleia davidii*) Zones 5-10

A plant that has the word "butterfly" in the name almost has to be included in a garden designed to attract insects with colorful wings. This shrub can grow quite large, however, and many people keep it in proportion with other plants by pruning it down hard every spring. Don't hesitate to cut a *Buddleia* down to around a foot tall...it will be five feet tall and flowering by the time your summer cocktail hour arrives. Deadheading improves the appearance and stimulates the production of new flowers, so don't hesitate to freshen up the party fare with some weekly snipping as the summer goes on.

POT MARIGOLD (*Calendula officinalis*) Annual in all zones

In hot areas, this annual is planted in the fall for winter flowering, and in cooler regions, it is grown in the spring and summer. It's worth including in any landscape, because birds, butterflies and bees are attracted to the flowers, and the edible blooms add color to both herb gardens and beverages.

GOLDENROD *(Solidago* spp.) Zones 3-9

No, goldenrod doesn't cause hay fever. Can't we put an end to that myth? This late-summer perennial comes in a variety of heights and flower styles, so there's sure to be a variety that will fit in your cocktail hour garden. Goldenrod is not only a native nectar source for butterflies, bees and wasps, but it's a lovely cut flower that is equally at home in a bouquet or as garnish on your salad!

JOE PYE WEED *(Eutrochium purpureum)* Zones 3-9

You'll need a large buffet table for this butterfly plant, but as long as your garden is big enough, this North American native brings height, nectar and color to the party. Formerly called *Eupatorium*, this pink-flowering perennial is an enthusiastic spreader, so just make sure that it doesn't hijack your garden.

GAY FEATHER *(Liatris spicata)* Zones 3-8

Who wouldn't want gay feathers and blazing stars (another common name) at their cocktail hour gathering, especially when this butterfly pleaser is also well behaved and easy to grow? Other than avoiding places where the soil stays soggy in the winter and finding a sunny area, this perennial makes few demands and adds a lovely, upright element to the garden.

MARIGOLDS *(Tagetes* spp.) Annual in all zones

Now don't be a snob...marigolds bring a great deal to the garden party. Mix them in with zinnias and salvia for a bed that is as colorful as a new box of crayons. Or, combine several types of marigolds together and create a flowerbed that's as vibrant as a Mexican fiesta or an Indian wedding. Those who are allergic to bee stings might want to include marigolds in their green hour gardens, because these flowers are attractive to butterflies but not to bees.

PENTAS *(Pentas lanceolata)* Zones 8-11

In colder regions, this is an annual, but in the warmth of zones 8 to 10, *Pentas* is a shrub. When used as an annual, the plant usually grows from a foot to two feet tall. Whether grown as a shrub or annual, this plant mingles well with perennials or other container plants, and pinching off the faded flowers helps keep the butterfly buffet well stocked.

'JEANA' AND VOLCANO® PHLOX *(Phlox paniculata* 'Jeana' or Volcano) Zones 3-8

While all varieties of *Phlox paniculata* might accurately be described as being attractive to bees and butterflies, I'm especially fond of 'Jeana' because it's long flowering and fairly shade tolerant as well. And if this isn't enough to include it on your menu for butterflies, consider that this perennial is very, very resistant to powdery mildew. The flowers are a bit smaller than on other varieties of summer phlox, but once you've had 'Jeana' at your cocktail hour celebration, you'll forget that you even considered inviting other tall selections.

When the butterfly buffet table needs shorter plants, however, look no further than volcano phlox.

This series of *Phlox paniculata* not only stay under three feet tall, but they rebound with a second set of huge, colorful blooms when deadheaded after the first round of flowering. In other words, as soon as the first course has been cleared from the butterfly banquet, the second course is placed on the table!

RUSSIAN SAGE *(Perovskia atriplicifolia)*
Zones 4-9

Although we think of this as a perennial, it's really a woody shrub. The silvery foliage and long period of bloom already makes it attractive for the people at your green hour, but butterflies will also appreciate finding this in the landscape. Russian sage mixes well with plants that have large foliage or flowers, and it pairs nicely with white blossoms.

VERBENA *(Verbena spp. and hybrids)*
Zone hardiness dependent on variety

There are many types of verbena with assorted characteristics. Suffice it to say that there are several that could be in the cocktail hour garden for butterfly refreshments. These flowering plants are particularly valuable in hot, dry locations, so if you've got a sunny slope or a hot-spot container garden, this is a go-to plant for you and the winged creatures you want to attract. But if you need a tall plant that's airy and will mix in with other flowering annuals and perennials, look no further than *Verbena bonariensis*, whose flowers are a butterfly (including monarch) magnet.

ZINNIAS *(Zinnia elegans* hybrids)
Annual in all zones

These annuals provide butterflies with nectar and a colorful, comfortable landing pad. Since they are native to Mexico, it's no wonder that zinnias are heat loving plants that have also naturalized in warmer parts of the United States. Because they have flat, horizontal surfaces, butterflies and bees can easily perch on these flowers while they enjoy the beverages you're serving.

Verbena bonariensis is a self-seeding annual or perennial, depending on your region, with tall, skinny stems that fit into many styles of gardens. The white cabbage butterfly almost looks like another flower when it perches on the purple flowers.

Good Hosts

A host plant supports butterflies during their larval stages, and like any good party host, they offer food that's appropriate to the occasion – and plenty of it. These plants don't have to grow in the cocktail hour garden, however, but can be planted anywhere on your property. Note that many larvae have very specific dietary restrictions, so if you want to support a particular type of butterfly, be sure to research the special diet that each specific insect requires.

BORAGE *(Borago officinalis)* **Annual in all zones**
A self-seeding herb that also attracts pollinators, borage has prickly foliage, so is most appreciated by people from afar. The painted lady butterfly doesn't mind the bristly leaves, however, so place this plant where the bees and painted ladies can mingle, but people are less likely to go.

CLOVER *(Trifolium* **spp.)** **Zones 3-9 when perennial**
There are several varieties of clover, and they provide food for varying species of butterfly larvae. Look for the types that will support butterflies in your region, and be prepared for the perennial species to self-seed in other parts of your landscape. Should you not want white clover in your lawn, don't invite this one into your yard. But should you want the lawn to be as wildlife friendly as the rest of your gardens, know that white clover makes an excellent companion to turf grasses.

DILL *(Anethum graveolens)* **Annual in all zones**
If the black swallowtail is on your preferred guest list, plant parsley and dill. You'll have herbs to cook with and host plants for swallowtail butterflies. Since dill can reseed, this is also a good plant to grow in a wildflower meadow or mix in with other host plants.

GOLDEN ALEXANDER *(Zizia aurea)* **Zones 3-8**
This is a perennial to plant just so you can say that there are "plants from A to Z" in your garden. But *Zizia* is also a lovely spring flowering perennial and an important food for the woodland swallowtail, making it a host that brings the most to your green hour party.

Golden Alexander flowers for a long time, grows in full sun or part shade and is important to a number of short-tongued insects and the black swallowtail butterfly larvae.

COMMON MILKWEED (*Asclepias syriaca*)
Zones 3-10

Poor milkweed. Although children have been charmed by setting the seed puffs free, and crafters have loved using the dried pods for art projects, the plant itself has usually been viewed as a common weed. Farmers spray it with herbicides to prevent it from mixing with their crops or being eaten by livestock. (The plant is poisonous to humans and animals.) Homeowners have routinely whacked it down or pulled it up, and although the seed pods were briefly seen as valuable in World War II, this *Asclepias*' familiar name says it all: we've regarded it as a common weed.

But since the sudden decline in monarch populations, *Asclepias syriaca* has been looked on with new eyes. People are now purchasing seeds and allowing it to mingle with standard flower garden plants and grasses. Because milkweed commonly blends with other plants on roadsides and in fields, it's a perennial that mixes well with other garden plants as well. Place this *Asclepias* anywhere on the property as a host plant for monarch larvae. The round, mauve flowers attract the winged creatures as well, so you just might want to have milkweed around during your cocktail hour.

Note that although you'll want milkweed to attend your green hour gathering, you wouldn't want it in the beverages that are served. The white sap that's in *Asclepias syriaca* is poisonous if ingested, although you'd have to eat a great deal of it to become really ill. It's also a skin irritant to some people, so *Asclepias* is best left to the butterflies. The toxicity of the sap actually serves to protect monarch larvae. The caterpillars sequester the toxic steroids, known as cardenolides, in milkweed sap, and these chemicals make the larvae poisonous to their predators.

WILD CHERRY (*Prunus serotina*) Zones 3-9

Here is a tree that supports more varieties of wildlife, including butterflies, than any other plant other than oaks, and most people treat them like trash. Get smart and invite some wild cherry trees to your property. The flowers are lovely, and many of these trees develop quirky shapes and a character that adds so much to the garden party.

These are just a few of the plants that support butterflies, and many species of these lovely insects depend on hosts that are native to local areas. Be sure to check with local sources for which butterflies and plants are linked in your region and plan accordingly for a truly green green hour.

Milkweed Goes to War

We understand how important the milkweed plant is for monarch butterflies, but did you know that the seeds in this plant also played an important role in American history? The fluff that disperses milkweed seeds by carrying them aloft on the slighted breeze has been historically used for stuffing mattresses and pillows. But during World War II, this plant became suddenly important for keeping people afloat instead of making seeds buoyant.

Before the war, life preservers, popularly known as "Mae Wests" after the well-endowed actress of the day, were commonly filled with kapok fiber. Kapok was taken from the seed fibers of the tropical kapok tree, *Ceiba pentandra*. The fluff that surrounds the *Ceiba* seeds is light in weight, resists water and was the most buoyant material available at the time for stuffing life vests.

But during the war, the Japanese took control of Indonesia where kapok fiber was harvested, forcing U.S. manufacturers of Mae Wests to scramble for another vest filler. The fluff that carries milkweed seeds off into the wind proved to be an acceptable substitute. Since the need for milkweed fibers was urgent, there was no time to cultivate crops that could be harvested for vest stuffing, so the call went out for private citizens to collect these seedpods.

Pamphlets were printed and distributed across the country calling for school children to gather milkweed pods. When collected before the cases could crack open and release their seeds, the husks served to protect the fluff and hold it when the pods were put into mesh bags. Children were given onion sacks and were told "Two

Milkweed pods and seeds are beautiful as they're illuminated in the late-day sun.

Bags Saves One Life" because two full sacks would stuff one Mae West jacket. The bags of pods were sent to a processing plant in Petoskey, Michigan, where the fibers were separated from the seeds and husks.

Millions of pounds of milkweed fluff were collected and processed by the end of the war. Although children have long been fascinated with the lighter-than-air milkweed fibers, we can imagine that during WWII they took even greater pleasure in knowing that by harvesting these seed pods, they had helped preserve human lives.

Party Planning:
A Recipe for Butterflies

- Find out which species of butterflies are most prominent in your area and do a search online to see which host plants are necessary for their survival, especially in their larval stages. Next, you can see if you already have these on your property. If not, plan to put them in place. Host plants do not have to be seen from your cocktail hour garden but can be placed in any location that's most convenient and fits in with your existing landscaping.

- Find which plants attract the butterflies themselves and integrate these into gardens that are easily seen from where you gather during the green hour. Even if these flowers are in containers or tucked among perennials or shrubs, you'll be able to watch the butterflies in flight from bloom to bloom.

- Those who want to get common milkweed established for the support of all phases of the Monarch butterfly will do well to first find some wild *Asclepias syriaca* and harvest some seed when the pods naturally split open. Milkweed seed needs to go through a chilling period in order to sprout, and the best way to provide this is how nature intended: the seeds need to spend the winter outside. Harvest seeds from milkweed pots and push them around on the top of the soil where you'd like them to grow. Don't cover with dirt, but make sure that the seeds are making contact with the ground so that they won't float away and can absorb moisture and push roots into the soil when germinating.

You are invited

∿∞

TO:

Feature Feathers and Flowers

WHERE:

In Your Yard & Garden

WHEN:

5 to 8 P.M.

RSVP:

To the Birds

Six

Attracting The Birds

One May afternoon, I pulled into my garage, got out of the car and began unloading groceries to carry into the house. As I was finishing this task, a buzzing, bumping sound caught my attention. There was a hummingbird in the garage, and it was flying in panic, crashing itself against the ceiling again and again, trying to get out. The open garage door was just a few feet away, but the bird was only focused upward, attempting to bash through the drywall.

First, I tried gently guiding the bird toward the door with a broom. This only made the poor thing more panicked and caused it to whack itself even harder. Next, I tried sending it mental messages to calm down and fly toward the light. "Go down, little bird, down. Only 16 inches lower." My powers as a bird whisperer clearly need improving, because the trapped creature didn't get the message. Finally, I went into the house in frustration; my distress was escalating along with the hummingbird's fright, and we both grew more upset every time it crashed into the ceiling.

Although my husband was on a ship off the coast of Norway at the time, when I emailed him about what was going on, he had the good sense to look the problem up online. "Put a vase of flowers near the door," he wrote back, "so that the bird will be attracted to that level." Although I was skeptical, I was willing to try anything. In the perennial garden, I picked fern leaf bleeding heart flowers and the *Lunaria* that I'd seen hummingbirds visit in the past. A few large tulips were added to act as flags that might capture the little bird's attention. I placed the

To lure the trapped hummingbird out of the garage and into the garden, I picked some of the flowers that I'd seen these birds feed on in the past. Would the panicked bird stop hitting itself on the ceiling long enough to notice the bleeding heart and other flowers? Incredibly, within a half hour, the tiny hummer was feeding on this bouquet, and from there it was a short flight out the door.

vase on the top of a shelf unit that was about three feet from the open door, and then I left the garage.

When I returned a half hour later, the hummingbird was next to the vase, dipping its beak into the *Lunaria* blooms. *Partial* success, I decided, and raised my cell phone to take a photo. The camera's clicking noise startled the bird, and it zipped straight away, through the open garage door and into the freedom of the outside world. *Total* success, even if I didn't manage to capture the bird's picture for my husband.

The take-home message for me that day was two-fold. First, now I know how to get a trapped hummingbird to go out instead of up. (Thanks, Dan!) Secondly, I realized that this bird could recognize a nectar source and start to feed within thirty minutes, *despite* its panic at being trapped in the garage. That tells us that a hummer is always on the lookout for food, so it shouldn't be too difficult for any of us to attract them to our decks or patios. All we need is the right flowers, and they don't have to be red. Birds belong in the cocktail hour garden, not in the garage, so start planting to make sure that they'll attend your outdoor gatherings where everyone will be happy.

Color, Motion and Personality

There are many reasons why we want birds around us during the green hour. Their feathers add flashes of color to all levels of the garden, from ground to shrub or tree to air. Sitting in the cocktail hour garden, you can be treated to ever-changing glimmers of reds, browns, blues, yellows and blacks. With birds flitting around the landscape, it might seem as if your flowers have taken flight.

One summer as my husband and I sat on our deck, we watched a blue jay and a Baltimore oriole chase each other around the yard. Back and forth they flew, first with the jay pursuing the oriole and then vice versa. It was blue vs. orange, the battle of the complementary colors!

We enjoyed watching this competition not only for the explosions of color but for the motion as well. Birds are especially valuable in the evening garden, because they come and go unpredictably. One night you might watch house wrens flying to and from their nesting box while feeding their young. On another evening you could see the dapper towhee hopping over the ground like a windup toy. The movement is constant and ever changing, and we enjoy it even more because of its randomness. What will be on show tonight?

Birds' characters are as diverse as their actions. Just as each dog and cat has its own personality, so too do the birds and other wildlife. Most of the time we don't notice the subtleties of wild animal behavior, but sitting in a cocktail hour garden is a time to appreciate the differences in behavior from one creature to the next. Even within the same species, individual birds exhibit diverse temperaments and individuality.

Attracting birds to the green hour garden adds to the richness of your evening experience. There are many ways to send invitations asking birds to join you during the green hour. Summon them in the manner that best suits your property, budget and the effort you wish to extend, then sit back and enjoy their presence.

Birdhouses are both functional and ornamental. This path at Massachusetts Horticultural Society's Elm Bank in Wellesley, MA, was lined with rustic poles and birdhouses, inviting adults and children to celebrate birds and shelter.

Cocktail Hour Birds

● As the sun sets, most birds find places of shelter. Some sleep in thickets and protected trees or bushes, while others find refuge in leaf piles, behind bark or in hollows of tree trunks. Many crowd together in trees or on the water, presumably because there is greater safety in numbers. Birds also roost under eaves, in open chimneys and in manmade roosting boxes. But unless they are sitting on eggs, they do not settle down in nests.

● Many birds have the ability to sleep with one eye open and half their brain on. This 50% sleep allows them to watch for danger while still getting some rest. Birds have the ability to control this unihemispheric slow-wave sleep, switching back and forth as needed. They can keep the eye that is closest to where danger might arise open, for example, or close both eyes when their situation seems more secure.

● When I first moved to Cape Cod, we lived a half mile from the ocean. As I was working in my perennial garden one evening, I happened to glance up at the sky. Flying past, over my garden, was a white and gray bird with a fish in its claws. Not only was it carrying a fish that was nearly as long as its body, but that fish was held face first, parallel to the bird. It looked as if the fish was swimming along, only a few inches under its captor. "Now that's something you don't see everywhere," I thought. Later I found out that I'd seen an osprey.

I also discovered that the osprey is unusual in that it has a reversible outer toe, which makes it possible to carry a fish in this manner. By turning a toe, they can hold their catch in a position that's aerodynamic, allowing the osprey to transport a rather large fish and still fly efficiently.

A birdhouse can provide a perfect focal point in a garden, because the hard materials are a visual relief from all of the plant textures. Woodworking artist Bobby Hallstein donated this beautifully crafted birdhouse to a non-profit's fundraiser.

Birdhouses

Some years ago a friend gave me a small white birdhouse that her spouse had made. Because it was mounted on a wooden stake about four feet tall, I decided it would make a good vertical ornament in a flower garden. But not knowing where I wanted to place this charming piece, I leaned it against the fireplace for a week while I made up my mind about placement. One evening, I was getting ready for the arrival of company and wanted the birdhouse out of my living room. Just to get it out of the way, and because I knew my guests would be outdoors having cocktails, I stuck it in the perennial border that surrounds the deck.

When my husband arrived home and began helping to carry snacks to the table on the deck, he saw this birdhouse placed behind the peonies. "Is that going to stay there?" he asked with *that tone* of voice that indicated he wasn't too happy about it. I replied that it was only in the garden for the night since I needed it out of the way. Then we both continued with our party plans.

The next morning when I went into the kitchen for coffee, my husband walked in from outside and said, "Well, you can't move that little white birdhouse. A bird began building a nest there this morning." When Dan went out at 6 a.m., he'd seen that a house wren had already started moving in.

That evening, as we sat on the deck, we watched the male perch on the roof of this birdhouse, singing with what we took to be complete joy. "Look at this great house I found," I imagined it was saying, "and in such a beautiful neighborhood! What a miracle it is that no one else discovered it first." Now we clean the birdhouse out every year and place it in that same location, where generations of young house wrens have been raised. My perennial garden is a beautiful neighborhood and I'm happy to share it with these tiny birds.

Birdhouses don't have to be as ornamental as the one that Bobby Hallstein made for my house wrens, and there are specific house sizes and shapes that attract particular birds. But know that some bird-houses are made as ornaments and others created with their future occupants in mind.

Look for birdhouses that are made from wood, because plastic or metal boxes can become too hot, especially when placed in sunny locations. The best nesting boxes have access to opening a side, top or bottom, because this allows for easy cleaning. Avoid houses that have a cute little perch in front of the opening; the birds that move in don't need such a resting place, but predator birds can make use of these to harass or harm the occupants inside.

Nesting Materials

There are many birds that aren't cavity dwellers but prefer to build nests in shrubs, trees, tall weeds on the ground or on top of your porch light. You can send invitations to these birds by providing a variety of nesting materials, and no, I'm not talking about that old notion of putting your dryer lint out in the bushes.

Birds appreciate natural ingredients, and every species of bird uses a different type of material. One might choose only twigs of a certain length, while a second prefers the soft tops from dried grasses. Some birds use a variety of stems and other plant matter, while others use a good amount of mud.

The problem is that we homeowners frequently clean up and cart off the very ingredients a bird might find most attractive. We prune dead twigs off our shrubs, rake up leaf litter, and cut down the grasses before their seed heads have broken off and blown away. This doesn't mean we have to leave our yards untended, but that we might recognize when some of the landscape clippings might make good nesting materials and set them aside for the birds.

Those who are feeling especially crafty can place such grasses, small twigs, fluffy seeds and pine needles into mesh containers and suspend them in places where the birds might easily find the ingredients they need. If you're in the mood for recycling, forget the dryer lint, which often has the remains of fabric softeners in it and absorbs water readily. Instead, use soft bits of yard, ribbons or small strips of soft cotton cloth. Save bits of garden materials as

Birds choose a variety of different materials to construct their nests. For some, it's a particular size and weight of twig. Others use fine grasses, while some birds choose bark, feathers or scraps of twine.

well, such as pieces of twine, burlap or even bits of old floating row cover.

Keep the hair that comes off the brush when you groom your dog or cat. Save the moss that comes on some flower arrangements or plant gifts and toss that in with materials you've collected in your spring or fall garden cleanup. Just keep the pieces fairly small and light; remember that a bird has to be able not only to extract the materials from the holder you've put them in but fly off to the nesting site with them as well.

Grow Your Own Shelter

Birds need places to shelter even when they aren't building nests. When you plant a diverse selection of shrubs, vines and trees, it can make a landscape more visually appealing while at the same time providing places of protection for winged wildlife. Birds need plants to perch in on their way to and from a feeder or water source. Such shrubs and trees give them a chance to assess these areas for possible danger before they swoop in for a snack or a drink.

Plants also provide refuge in bad weather. Birds will seek out congested foliage that is out of the wind so that they have a sanctuary during storms. Although most of us don't actually plan our yards and gardens to provide bird havens, knowing that birds appreciate a varied range of shrubs and trees on all sides of our homes is another reason to plant with diversity in mind.

It's also another purpose for keeping our plants as full and healthy as possible. We want to encourage thickly growing shrubs for our own aesthetic reasons, but it's satisfying to know that a full plant is also good for sheltering the birds we enjoy watching during the green hour.

When a nest is made out in the open and at human eye level, you'd think that the babies would be more vulnerable, but the parent bird seemed to know that a cactus would offer great protection. There are a few birds, including the cactus wren, that construct their nests among thorny plants.

Drinks and a Bath

What is a good nest without easy access to a refreshing drink and cleansing bath? Just as we humans look for hotels that have a bathroom and a mini-bar, birds appreciate having their facilities close at hand. Dripping water always attracts birds, so if water isn't scarce in your area, set up a low rock or stone with a depression where birds can drink and a slow drip that will attract them. Where a small amount of water remains from day to day, adding a product made of *Bacillus thuringiensis israelensis* will kill mosquito larvae but not hurt the birds. This variety of Bt is sold at most garden centers and many home stores.

You don't need a feeder to attract birds to your cocktail hour garden. Fresh water and a frequently cleaned birdbath will lure these colorful, winged animals to your green hour gatherings.

Birdbaths function as both drinking and bathing stations, and for this reason should have the water changed frequently. If your life doesn't accommodate a daily changing of birdbath water, find another way to invite birds to your cocktail parties.

The shape of a birdbath is important, and shallow is better than deep. Birds want to know that when they go into a basin of water for bathing, they aren't going to slip into "the deep end." Although most birds can swim, many prefer not to. Water that's about two inches deep and a birdbath that isn't slick but offers sure footing, is perfect.

Landscape designer Don Milbier knows that dripping water always attracts birds, so in his own yard he set up a birdbath with a slow drip feature.

Grow Your Own Birdfeeder

Of course you can attract birds to your property with feeders filled with seed. But with the right plants, you can feed the birds without buying birdseed. Because the bird populations vary so greatly from region to region, the plants that support wildlife in each area differ, too. Request recommendations for regional natives at your local garden center, and be sure to place an assortment of native plants in the landscape.

In most areas of the country, you can also plant annual sunflowers, tickseed *(Coreopsis)*, gayfeather *(Liatris)* and black-eyed Susans *(Rudbeckia)* for the birds to feast on. Include several native varieties that are recommended for birds in your region. And be sure to let the stalks remain in the garden well into the fall, waiting until spring to cut the dead stalks down. Many perennial plants, including purple coneflower *(Echinacea purpurea)*, have seed-heads that are visually attractive to people and also provide a culinary treat for birds.

Plant coneflowers and you not only have a butterfly magnet, you've got birdfeeders as the flowers go by. Many birds eat *Echinacea* seeds, so don't clip off the wilted flowers if you'd like to watch the birds flit in and around the plants.

Just for Fun
Build Your Own Bowerbird Nest

A fun early spring project is to make your own nest using natural materials, a glue gun and assorted colorful ribbons. These make pretty centerpieces that celebrate the season of rebirth.

In Australia and New Guinea, bowerbirds are famous for their elaborate courtship behavior. The male bird will build a nest structure and decorate the entrance with an assortment of natural and found objects in an attempt to attract a mate. These objects are often colorful and manmade.

Bowerbird nests might be surrounded by colored clothespins stolen from a clothesline, bits of colorful plastic or even candy wrappers. Often a bird will show a preference for a particular color, so nests are found surrounded by only blue or red objects, for example.

As I read about these remarkable birds, I thought, "Why should the birds have all the fun?" Making your own nest can be an enjoyable creative project. All you need is a selection of twigs, moss, pine needles and grasses, a glue gun and whatever colorful additions suit your fancy.

Hummingbirds Top the A-list

When it comes to cocktail hour birds, hummingbirds are the most sought after guests at every evening gathering. They are so svelte, well dressed and charming, who wouldn't want them at their party? And their quick and graceful dance moves, as they hover by one flower or zip off to seek others, are always entrancing.

Some put up feeders that hold sugar water to attract hummingbirds, but I prefer to serve them the real thing: nectar-rich plants. Here are a few annuals and perennials that will pull in the hummers.

BEARDTONGUE *(Penstemon* sp.)
Zone 4-10 depending on variety

Penstemons range from short to tall and come in a wide variety of colors and zone hardiness. What remains constant throughout the genus, however, is their love of full sun and good drainage. Heavy, damp soils and places that flood in the winter are the kiss of death for these plants, so think sand, slopes and dry feet for any of the beardtongues.

Even in the best of conditions, they aren't long-lived perennials, so when they flourish, expect them to stick around the party for three to five years before vanishing.

BEE BALM *(Monarda* sp.) Zones 4-9

Perhaps this plant should be called the-birds-and-the-bees-balm, although we'd risk offending the butterflies by leaving them out. In any case, *Monarda* has been a standard in perennial gardens because it

Don't assume that all coral or red flowers attract hummingbirds. Some aren't good nectar sources. Most *Agastache* varieties, however, routinely lure the hummers in.

flowers in mid-summer, tolerates clay soils and is a favorite nectar source for hummingbirds. In areas where plants get powdery mildew, look for the tall variety called 'Jacob Cline', since it is more resistant than other varieties.

Red cardinal flower (*Lobelia cardinalis*) is a hummingbird favorite. It's also a perennial that self-seeds gently in landscapes, providing bright red exclamation points against green foliage.

CARDINAL FLOWER (*Lobelia cardinalis*)
Zones 4-8

Hummingbirds love this plant, so perhaps it's responsible for the myth that they prefer red flowers. In any case, these North American native perennials provide tall exclamation point dashes of color that add excitement to most gardens. These plants self-seed where happy and appreciate damp soils, so these hummingbird lures are perfect for those wet spots where rain collects or drainage is poor.

CALIFORNIA FUCHSIA (*Epilobium* sp.)
Zones 5-9 depending on variety

Another common name for *Epilobium* is hummingbird trumpet, so if you're able to grow this plant get ready to strike up the band. These plants are heat tolerant and they don't drink much, so they are perfect for the xeric beds and borders. Be aware that some California fuchsia (formerly called *Zauschneria*) are a bit slow to get growing, and others can have fragile stems. They make good container plants, and many are also well suited for draping over walls.

FLOWERING SAGE (*Salvia* sp.)
Zones 3-10 depending on variety

There is a flowering *Salvia* for every garden party. Many that are only hardy in very warm climates make good summer annuals, and many are hummingbird favorites. In my garden, *Salvia* 'Black and Blue' is a hummingbird magnet, and although it's not reliably perennial in my warm zone 6, the summer-long flowering makes it worth planting as an annual. Look for varieties with trumpet-shaped flowers, as these are usually good nectar plants.

HUMMINGBIRD MINT (*Agastache* sp.)
Zones 6-10 depending on variety

Sometimes the common name says it all. *Agastache* plants can be grown as annuals or used as reliable perennials where hardy, but they are all great for luring hummingbirds to your green hour. Use several in flowerbeds and mixed containers, and your A-list guests will even arrive unfashionably early.

Party Planning:
Bring In the Birds

- Use as many native shrubs and trees as possible. If some aren't as ornamental as you'd like for the green hour garden, plant them in side yards, on the perimeters or at the back of your property. Use a few native plants as the bee/bird/butterfly backbone to the landscape.

- Keep bird feeders and baths as clean as possible. Once you have a feeder and birdbath, you understand where the expression "dirty bird" comes from. There are several enzyme-based cleaners available for use in cleaning bird basins and feeding stations.

- When planning for attracting hummingbirds, place some spring blooming plants that are nectar sources in your landscape so that the birds have food as soon as they arrive. Azaleas, bleeding heart, columbine, lilacs and flowering quince are just a few plants that will add color to your spring garden and help convince the hummingbirds to stick around for the summer cocktail hour gatherings.

Unwind after that stressful drive home from work with the help of the avian wildlife. Birds add color and motion to any garden. For example, watching a red bird such as this cardinal come and go in the evening can be extremely soothing.

You are invited

TO:

An Elemental Experience

WHERE:

In Your Yard & Garden

WHEN:

5 to 8 P.M.

RSVP:

To Earth, Air, Fire and Water

Seven

Conversations with Earth, Air, Fire, Water and Sky

*E*ven if there is only one person at your green hour, there are several conversations going on – like a lively cocktail party. The discussions may not be happening person to person but are occurring between your five senses and the five elements. If you pay attention, you'll realize that earth, air, fire, water and sky are chatting with you through touch, taste, smell, sight and sound. And when you get a group of such spirited guests together, some of the talk will be light or frivolous, while other exchanges will be intensely personal and deep-rooted.

When planning your cocktail hour garden, think about the ways that your senses communicate with the elements. Some of these will automatically be included as any garden is created. We touch the soil as plants are put in place and inhale the perfume of fragrant flowers. We hear the birds call and taste herbs that are growing nearby.

But other communications between the elements and our senses need to be purposefully planned. Many of these chats will be extremely subtle, which is all the better, because a noisy party can quickly become chaotic and tiresome. As you plan for your green hour garden, ask yourself this question: What if the five elements got together with the five senses and began to have conversations about garden design?

Earth

Touch

Thinking about the importance of touching soil reminds me of my mother. When she became physically disabled and needed to move to assisted living, she took all of her houseplants with her. Even so, Mom greatly missed working in her garden. One spring she said to me, "There's just something about this season that makes everyone here want to go dig in the dirt."

The desire to plant is deeply ingrained in our psyches. Perhaps it's embedded after centuries of *Homo sapiens* working the earth in order to grow crops. Or maybe we instinctually know that having our skin in contact with the soil is as important as the food we've cultivated.

There is a mounting recognition that the populations of microbial species in our bodies play a large role in maintaining good health. And some of these beneficial bacteria are transmitted into our bodies by handling the soil. Even if this has no role in our desire to play in the dirt, it's interesting to reflect that gardening cultivates good health because we are literally in touch with the earth.

Sight

For many people, connecting with the earth through sight might be more pleasurable than getting dirt under their fingernails. In the cocktail hour garden, there are numerous ways that we stay grounded through what we see.

ROCKS. Rocks are often attractive additions to any garden, and in the green hour landscape they can serve a variety of functions. We spoke in Chapter 5 about the importance of providing warming stations for butterflies. While rocks are a natural source of heat stored from the sun, rocks in a garden also serve an important design function by adding visual weight to a landscape filled with the fine textures of foliage.

Rocks have actual weight, of course, but their large surfaces provide the perfect contrast with all of the

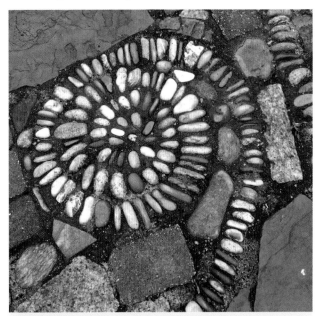

What better way to celebrate the elements than with a patchwork stone flooring for your green hour garden. This area combines recycled cement blocks, stone countertop scraps, slate, cobblestones and beach rocks that are held in place with polymeric sand.

small leaves that fill most landscapes. For this reason, the bigger the rocks are, the better they look in a landscape. Some people are fortunate enough to have large stones in their yards and gardens naturally, but others need to purchase them. The smart garden designer doesn't just place the imported rock on the top of the soil, however, but buries it at least halfway. Sinking rocks into the ground makes them look as if they've always been there instead of being trucked in and plopped down at random.

In most landscapes, rocks are best when placed in groups instead of in lines, unless, of course, they are used to build up walls. Flat stones can be made into paths or patios; all of these provide the solid materials that give a garden a natural, attractive distinction.

BERMS OR BURIAL MOUNDS?

When starting a new garden, many homeowners are tempted to create a berm and plant on top of that pile of soil. Some want to give their plants a boost of a foot or more of instant height, while others think that adding some changes in their yard's topography might make things more interesting. Unfortunately, many people don't consider that there's an appropriate visual scale when adding swells of earth.

Hills that are too high end up looking

like miniature volcanoes or mountain ridges that erupt plants. Functionally, those high mounds are also harder to plant, weed or mulch. There is also a watering issue – it's difficult to maintain a consistent level of moisture since the moisture runs off. And since a larger surface area is exposed to the air, these areas dry more quickly. If a berm is made too small, it looks more like a burial mound or grave than a natural change in the flow of the land.

Smaller mounds end up confining shrub or tree roots to an undersized area, creating reduced support systems that ultimately lead to a weaker plant. Visually, small mounds of soil look like just what they are: a load of dirt dumped on an otherwise flat garden. Are you getting the impression that I'm not in favor of an artificial hill of earth? Both functionally and aesthetically, a berm only makes sense when it's wide enough and sufficiently low to look as if it's the natural flow of the land.

Beyond actual dirt and rocks, however, there are other ways to remind us of the earth. Terra-cotta flowerpots are made from a material that looks just like what it is: clay from the ground. A group of terra-cotta pots filled with plants is one conversation starter between the earth and your sense of sight.

Smell

If there's a space by your cocktail hour garden that's under cover, be sure to spend time there during a rainfall. The fragrance of wet earth is such a pleasing scent, and most of us forget to indulge in a deep breath of the earth's perfume.

Taste

No, I'm not suggesting that you eat dirt. But there are flavors you can include in your cocktail hour that have an earthy quality that can start a conversation about the connections between the ground and our taste buds. Beets are probably the best-known food that can have an earthy flavor, especially when they are scrubbed clean, left unpeeled and put through a juicer. Consider using unconventional vegetable garden plants in your cocktails or as garnish for the drinks.

When the porch is covered, the cocktail hour doesn't have to move indoors just because of a driving rain. This front entry is the perfect place for green hour gatherings in stormy weather. In this area, the rain chain, normally used to direct water from a roof or gutter, has been planted with succulents and used as garden ornament instead of for its normal function.

Landscaping very breezy areas can include plantings of shrubs and trees that will slow the winds somewhat. This planting, which includes bayberry *(Myrica pensylvanica)*, Virginia sweetspire *(Itea virginica)*, and arrowwood Viburnum *(Viburnum dentatum)*, is an example of using a variety of native plants that look natural and attractive while providing a wind break.

Air

Touch

There are two times when our sense of the air in a garden is especially important: when we're too hot and when there is too much wind. In hot weather, we welcome a breeze, but when the wind is blowing too much, we quickly feel battered and exhausted by the gusts.

The design of the evening garden should consider both possibilities, depending on the landscape's location. On city rooftop gardens, by the ocean or in other places where it's likely to be windy, the addition of a windbreak can provide the shelter that makes the difference between a pleasurable evening and weathering the gale. Such barriers can be made from a line of plants, fencing or a glass panel that stops the wind while preserving a view.

By the same token, putting up a wall or a line of shrubs that blocks the gusts doesn't make sense in places where every breeze is welcome. And a light wind doesn't just refresh us when the temperatures are warm, they also blow mosquitoes and other insects away. So before you place taller plants or fencing in locations that might seem advantageous for privacy, consider that these barriers might end up obstructing useful and pleasing breezes as well.

Grasses not only catch the light but the breezes as well, adding motion to the garden.

Smell

Fragrance and breezes are natural cocktail hour partners. Light winds bring the perfume from nearby flowers and foliage into our green hour spaces. When you've included fragrant plants in your garden design and containers, you'll be treated to wafts of perfume when the breeze blows.

Sight

Motion is an important part of every garden, but when people design garden spaces they sometimes forget to include plants that shift in the wind. Fine grasses and perennials with long, slender stems are as important for adding movement to the cocktail hour garden as they are for catching the rays of the setting sun. Look for plants that are especially breeze-worthy such as Mexican feather grass *(Nassella tenuissima)* and wandflower *(Gaura lindheimeri)*.

But the cocktail party conversation between the elements and senses doesn't have to end with plants that move in the breezes. Another playful way to bring this element into the green hour garden is with a display of air plants. These are plants in the genus *Tillandsia* that seemingly live on air alone, although we know that this isn't really accurate.

Tillandsia are epiphytes that absorb water and nutrients through their leaves. They usually live on trees and often have colorful flowers. Some *Tillandsia* flowers are even fragrant. In many ways, these sculptural-looking epiphytes are the perfect conversation starter between the elements and the senses.

Celebrate air and light with some sculptural *Tillandsia* plants. Frequently called air plants, these epiphytes don't need soil. They do require filtered light, misting or splashing with water three times a week and good air circulation. If you want to encourage flowering, mix a weak concentration of orchid fertilizer in your watering can or mister.

Fountains can provide the sound of a waterfall while complimenting the style of the garden. This fountain in Thomas Hobbs's former garden in Vancouver is a structure that provides color and sound and is the perfect complement the colorful blend of perennials and succulents in the beds.

The talents of stone artist Lew French and landscape designer Carly Look joined together to create this lovely garden on Martha's Vineyard. The rocks are deliberately placed so as to appear as if they have been in those locations for decades.

Sound

Air converses with us in the cocktail hour garden through the rustling of foliage, the harmonies from wind chimes or the ringing of bells. All of these can be easily incorporated into the evening garden depending on your preferences. The sounds we each find soothing are very personal.

If the swishing of stems and leaves is your idea of good cocktail hour chatter, plant a heavenly bamboo shrub *(Nandina domestica)*, any of the tall grasses or a true clump bamboo *(Fargesia)* in the garden. Birch leaves are also known for the rustling sound they make in the wind, and most other trees swish with enough of a breeze.

WIND CHIMES. Some people love the sound of wind chimes in a garden, but it's advisable to listen to a set before you make the purchase. Wind chimes can have high rings, low rings and be tuned to several different keys. The set that appeals to one ear might sound cacophonous to another. You can also make your own wind chimes using just about any materials. They can be colorful, whimsical or very natural. Wind chimes can be made from old kitchen utensils, bells, seashells or pieces of wood. Any object that can be suspended from a string and knock together in the breezes can be made into a combination chime and ornament.

Another way to celebrate wind is by hanging bells or wind chimes in the garden. Some ring with the slightest of breezes, while others will need a gust of gale strength to make them chime. Choose the type of bell or chime according to how often you'd like wind to contribute to the cocktail hour conversation.

The Elements of a Good Cocktail

Like a really good meal, a good cocktail should be seasonal, flavorful and attractive. It should appeal to your senses of sight and smell as well as taste. Some general guidelines include the following:

- **A LITTLE SUGAR OR OTHER SWEETENING** is important for many cocktails. The touch of sweet blends other flavors together. Many classic cocktails use simple syrup for this purpose. A simple syrup is one part sugar to one part water, boiled and cooled. But there are other ways to add sweetness without the calories, and other, more complex flavors. Maple syrup is especially good in drinks made with brown liquors such as bourbon or dark rum. Agave syrup is a bit sweeter than sugar, so you'd use less in a drink recipe. This sweetener is popular in summer cocktails, like mojitos and margaritas. There are also simple syrups available that are made with the herb stevia, or you can experiment with growing the herb and crushing it in your drinks for a zero-calorie sweetening option.

- **FLAVORS OF THE SEASON** are as valuable in a beverage as they are on the table. Think strawberries in the early spring, watermelon, peaches and blueberries in the summer or beets and pears in the fall. Feel free to experiment with adding fresh vegetables, too.

- **STAYING BALANCED IS VITAL.** A general recipe is two ounces of spirits (this can be two separate types), one ounce of simple syrup or equivalent sweetening and three-quarters to one ounce of a sour flavor such as lemon or lime. Pre-made cocktail mixers usually have the sweet and sour elements together in correct proportions. Those who love mixing a fresh drink from scratch, however, will want to use fresh citrus and the sweetener of their choice. For non-alcoholic cocktails, replace the spirits with a liquid that is flavorful but not sweetened.

- **ICE HELPS** to chill a cocktail and lighten it up. Before-dinner drinks should be light and refreshing in the summer and warmer in the winter, but never heavy, overly alcoholic or too filling.

- **EXPERIMENT AND HAVE FUN.**  Play with different flavor combinations. Use fragrant plants for garnishes so that you'll inhale their scent just as you begin to taste the drink. Pick edible flowers for the glass or pitcher and try all types of herbs. Putting together a drink is a great deal like making a meal or planting a garden. Start with the basic guidelines and then make it your own.

Fire

Sight and Sound

Touch may be stand-offish about fire, and Smell tends to appreciate a whiff of smoke from a distance but not at close range. Taste, of course, might only be interested if hotdogs on a stick or s'mores are involved. Nevertheless, people do love to gather around a few burning logs, watching the flames and listening to them crackle and pop.

Where you choose to add the element of fire to your cocktail hour garden depends on the space you have, the style of your home and property and even the region where you live. Fire pits and fireplaces that are safe and frequently used in one part of the country might be unwise because of drought in another region.

If actual fires are prohibited or just not practical in your landscape, consider making reference to flames by using hot-colored plants. Try the spiky, flame-

This delightful fire pit area at Windy Hill demonstrates that patios can be a part of the garden itself. Carol Pledger and Paul Spector's patio blends seamlessly into the flower borders of their country-style flowerbeds.

shaped flowers of red *Salvia*, for example, or the torch-shaped blooms of the poker plant (*Kniphofia* sp.) to add heat to your plantings without an actual blaze.

Water

Sight and Sound

Ask anyone what they picture when they think of a very relaxing vacation, and they're likely to say something like, "Sitting at a beach, doing nothing but looking at the ocean." There is something extremely calming about seeing and hearing a body of water. This is what draws vacationers to ocean and lakesides and what pulls us to waterfalls and rushing rivers.

Since most people aren't blessed by waterfront property, the next best thing is to incorporate water features into our yards and gardens. They can provide a touch of the same tranquility that we feel at a shore.

This is one of the original ponds that John Sullivan designed for his exuberant gardens on Cape Cod. It is a great demonstration that a water feature can fit in with any style of planting, from a bright flower garden to a serene moss garden done in an Asian style and everything in between.

From ponds and waterfalls to fountains, the sounds and sights of water can easily be arranged for every cocktail hour landscape.

Backyard pools can be just about any size, shape and design. The sound of falling water is created with a pump – in a waterfall, a fountain or in the center of a pond. Some homeowners design water features that are large enough to hold aquatic plants and fish, while others prefer to create pondless waterfalls.

The limiting factors when creating such water features are primarily budget and space, although maintenance and local regulations about fencing around pools should be factored in as well. Although it's possible for a homeowner to design and build their own waterfall or pool, be sure to research this well and talk with others who are either professional landscapers who specialize in aquatic work or gardeners who've done something similar themselves.

Small fountains can provide the sound of running water without major construction, and there are plug-in and fill units available in many lovely styles. From formal and classic to cute or kitschy, there's a type for every landscape situation. Wall fountains can be hung on buildings, and freestanding units can be placed on decks or balconies and turned on as the spirit moves.

Sky

If you're fortunate enough to have a view of the western sky from your green hour garden, be sure not to plant large trees that will ultimately block the spectacle of the setting sun.

Sight

In some cultures, the fifth element is the sky and represents the heavens and things beyond the mundane. This fifth element is a crown to our green hour garden that stretches into infinity and converses most with our sense of sight. One of the pleasures of mid-summer cocktail hours is to watch the movement of clouds and the play of light across the sky. Viewing the constantly-shifting cloud patterns and transformations of colors as the sun sets can be as soothing as watching the waves on the ocean.

In order to leave parts of the cocktail hour garden open to the sky, be sure not to surround the space with shrubs and trees that will grow so large that upward views will be blocked. And, if your green hour garden is already covered by a porch ceiling, consider painting it blue. Sky blue has been a traditional color for porch ceilings in Southern states, and it has been long-favored for Victorian style homes as well.

Party Planning: Elements and Style

● When designing with earth, wind, fire, water and sky, it's best to start with the style of your architecture and overall landscape and use that to begin your conversations with the senses. Asian-style rock sculptures might not be the best choice for a New England country garden, for example. Fountains, fire pits and other garden ornaments usually look best when there is a continuity of design in the landscape and a match of style and the garden's location.

● Some sounds and fragrances are all the more delightful because they are subtle. Give these experiences a chance to make themselves known. If you want to hear the soft rustling of bamboo or grasses, don't also hang wind chimes in the area. Or if you'd enjoy the wafting of scents from flowers or foliage, don't burn citronella-scented candles in the garden.

● Before constructing water or fire features, check regional rules having to do with safety issues, including the fencing of ponds and pools or the burning of wood in pits or fireplaces, etc. Some of these features may need to be kept at a certain distance from the property lines. Each municipality has its own regulations about such constructions, and it's better to know in advance if there are limits or restrictions on these landscape features.

A chiminea waits to be fired up on a chilly summer evening on a Nantucket patio. The gardens that surround this area are a colorful mix of self-seeding annuals and perennials, masterfully planted by Chris Hestwood and maintained by Chris and her husband, Bob.

You are invited

TO:

The Grazing Garden

WHERE:

In Your Vegetable Beds

WHEN:

5 to 8 P.M.

RSVP:

To Edible Plants

Eight

The Green Hour Vegetable Garden: Cocktail Hour Grazing

In a casual evening gathering with friends, where are we most likely to be found? In which room of the house will your guests end up sipping drinks, chatting and nibbling on snacks? In the kitchen, of course. So why should a garden get-together be any different? Kitchens and kitchen *gardens* are places of nourishment, creativity and hospitality. Come on in and make yourself at home.

The New Veggie Garden

The days of hiding vegetable gardens in the back of the property are so last century, for several worthy reasons. First of all, many backyards just aren't as large as those common in the early to mid-1900s. Back in the days when a backyard could be well over

a half acre, often with an alley running behind for maintenance vehicles, it was typical to place fruits and vegetables in the rear of a property. Plots are now smaller, and the size of an entire lot may be a quarter acre or less.

When yards were larger, you would likely have areas in the rear that enjoyed plenty of sunlight. Since vegetables grow best when they receive at least six hours of dead-on sun, that's where a garden was located. But with a smaller property, you might have much of your backyard shaded by a neighbor's trees. In such situations, the front yard or the side of the house might be the only location where there is sufficient sunlight to grow vegetables.

But beyond the changes in lot size and the necessities created by sun and shade, there has been a shift in how we think about garden styles in general and vegetable gardens in particular. In the past, many landscapes tended to look just like the neighboring properties, with little variation from house to house when it came to landscape styles. Some communities mandated a certain "look" and detailed which styles or approaches to planting were not allowed. Such zoning regulations and neighborhood association rules still exist in some areas.

Over the past thirty years, it's become more acceptable for property owners to use individual landscaping styles. Throughout the country, people have challenged laws that either prohibit front yard vegetable gardens or require large stretches of front lawn. For many homeowners, the front yard is the most open and sunny area they have, and naturally they want to place their veggie gardens there.

This has become more tolerated and even embraced, as people have new appreciation for local, fresh food. At the same time, they are aware that there are many ways to design, plant and maintain vegetable gardens so that the veggie plots are as attractive as any flowerbed, and therefore worthy for putting "on display" in all parts of a landscape.

Vegetables do not have to be grown in straight rows in rectangular spaces unless the owner of the garden finds this the most pleasing planting style. Some may want to plant in patches, squares or other shapes instead of rows. And others might choose to grow their vegetables in raised beds or containers.

Some kitchen gardens are crisply styled and meticulously maintained, while others are constructed of recycled materials and planted more loosely. There are raised beds, rectangular plots and circular or serpentine gardens. Certain gardens are prettily flower-filled, whereas others have attitude. There is no right way. Find the style that fits in with the rest of your landscape and house. Think about which style speaks to your mind and soul and then start planting.

Raised beds have become popular in landscapes because they offer a way to delineate the vegetable garden while providing quickly amended soil that supports the growth of closely-placed plants. When such beds are high enough, they also allow tending without getting on your hands and knees, so they are a good option for people who have difficulty getting up and down.

Containers offer a means of growing edibles on decks, balconies and patios. They allow people to take advantage of small sunny areas that would otherwise be difficult to cultivate. And some gardeners like to raise their produce in containers because it keeps their crops out of reach of rabbits and other critters.

The New Garden in the Green Hour

This trend in flexible, edible landscaping is important for the cocktail hour garden because, frankly, it offers a greater choice in party venues. A landscape for relaxation that appeals to all the senses will please our eyes and our taste buds, so there is no reason that green hour rituals shouldn't take place in a garden that's a mixture of ornamental and edible or in an area of the landscape solely devoted to vegetables. We've become accustomed to seeing tables in an apple orchard or vineyard...why not in a vegetable garden, too?

When we bought the land at Poison Ivy Acres, we knew that the vegetable garden would need to go in our front yard, and that we would need to take down the few black locust trees (*Robinia pseudoacacia*) that grew there. Knowing that the old timers in the area say that "Black locust posts last one year longer than cement," Dan decided to use the trunks and branches from those trees to create this fence. The flowers that surround this garden attract a host of pollinators, and the arbor beckons us into the center of the garden during the green hour.

These cherry tomatoes provide a splash of color to the garden, and a satisfying cocktail hour snack as well.

Grazing in the veggie patch has been a long tradition among vegetable gardeners. When grown organically, there are many vegetables and fruits that can be picked right from the plant and popped directly into the mouth. So, some cocktail hour snacks can be savored on the spot, "farm to mouth."

Since sugar snap peas and cherry tomatoes are usually supported and bear fruit well above the ground, in organic gardens these can be consumed without washing. Bush beans that hold the crops off the soil can also be good for serving up cocktail hour snacks that require no plates. It's not only novel to pick your hors d'oeuvres right before you bite into them, but the flavor that freshly harvested vegetables and fruits contain surpasses any produce that you can buy, even that sold at a farmers' market.

But instant gratification aside, there are other reasons for taking the cocktail party into the vegetable garden or inviting the veggies into your green hour landscape. There is something positively soul-satisfying about gathering close to where our food is growing. It is the appeal of a meal overlooking a vine-yard or a farm-to-table dinner set right in the fields of produce. Just the sight of growing crops nourishes our spirits and reconnects our awareness to the importance of the land. Fortunately, there are many ways to combine your vegetables and the cocktail hour garden.

Just for Fun...
Fresh From the Garden Cocktail Hour Snacks

If grazing right off the plants isn't your thing, or if it seems appropriate to be a bit fancier when entertaining in the garden, consider these cocktail hour snacks that can be prepared just before the guests arrive.

PEAPODS AND DIP
Replace the usual chips with fresh sugar snap or snow peas. You can use the packaged or pre-prepared dip of your choice, or make your own healthy version using non-fat Greek yogurt, coarse mustard, finely chopped fresh herbs, and red or black pepper and salt to taste.

RADISH ROSES
Wash radishes picked from the garden and slice a thin piece off the top and bottom. Next, slice around them, not quite through, moving around the radish and cutting a quarter part of the peel so that you have four "petals." Some people make these by making four or five slices all across the radish, but not deep enough to cut through, and then doing another set of four or five perpendicular to the first. Place the radishes in ice water for three or more hours so that the "petals" open up.

NASTURTIUM WRAPS
Round nasturtium leaves make wonderful, tiny green taco-shaped finger food wrappings. Because the leaves have a slight spiciness, they complement a creamy filling. Pick leaves that are about two inches in diameter. Wash them if they're sandy and snip off any stem pieces close to the leaf. Place them stem side up on a plate or cutting board and place a teaspoon of the filling of your choice on each leaf. Cream cheese mixed with cumin or chili powder to taste is good, especially when a small amount of the hot sauce of your choice is added. Or try hummus and goat cheese, or a soft goat cheese and olive paste. Fold the leaf over to complete the wrap, chill and serve.

Fresh sugar-snap peas and nasturtium leaf wraps filled with goat cheese and olives are perfect cocktail hour snacks in the vegetable garden. You might not want to go inside for dinner.

Veggie Garden Furnishings

One simple way of spending your green hour in the vegetable garden is to add seating, just as you would on a deck or patio. Larger vegetable gardens might accommodate a table or a grouping of chairs in the center or sides of the beds themselves. In smaller areas, benches can be placed in or around the vegetables.

Veggie garden furnishings don't necessarily have to be permanent. There are many fold-up bistro tables and chairs that can be opened and used in the garden when needed. These can be placed outside the garden when necessary in order to tend the vegetables using wheelbarrows or garden carts or when setting sprinklers for watering. But at the end of the day, when it's

There is no better place to celebrate the green hour than in the vegetable garden. Make a garden-based beverage such as these blueberry cocktails, pick some snow peas or fresh green beans and add the dip of your choice. Put aside your digital devices and savor the abundance around you.

time to stop working and count your garden blessings, the furniture can be unfolded and quickly put into service.

When planning a new vegetable garden, consider making a seating area that is a permanent part of the design. Such spaces are not only useful for the green hour but as a place to rest while tending the vegetables, doing veggie cleanup such as snapping ends off of green beans or perching with a cup of coffee in the morning.

Raised Glasses Among Raised Beds

If you prefer to grow your vegetables in raised beds, there are ways to combine this style of growing with a cocktail hour space. Consider creating two raised beds that run parallel to each other placed six to eight feet apart. The space in between those two beds could be made into a patio area with pavers or simply mulched with gravel or bark mulch. Add seating and pots of herbs and you have an instant cocktail hour garden set among your vegetable beds.

In fact, if a patio is already located in a sunny area, think about constructing your raised beds around the perimeter of the existing hardscape. Gardens that are closer to the house might be easier to tend, and they are certainly more convenient for quickly harvesting a salad right before dinner.

When raised beds are made high enough, the timbers themselves can function as informal cocktail hour seating. Taller beds are especially convenient for anyone who can't easily get up and down, since they can be tended by sitting on the edge of the framework and leaning into the garden from both sides. The sides of these beds can occasionally accommodate people and beverages, as long as they're relatively free of soil.

Containing the Green Hour

If there isn't space for a full veggie garden or even raised beds, the green hour gardener can turn to container gardening and use pots and boxes. The key to success here is to choose the largest containers you can, especially when growing larger plants such as tomatoes. Be sure to fill vegetable garden containers with only soil; no rocks, mulch or other filler should be used, and nothing should cover the drainage holes.

Must-have cocktail hour treats in the Fornari garden include Maxibel green beans, Sun Gold cherry tomatoes and nasturtium rollups. These nasturtium leaves were filled with a mix of cream cheese, walnuts and nasturtium flowers.

Smaller Edibles for Containers

The following fruits and vegetables are just a few of the varieties that have been bred for container vegetable gardening. Although many of these plants may look small when you plant them, don't crowd several in a pot. If their roots are crowded, the growth and production of fruit or vegetables up above will be diminished.

RASPBERRY SHORTCAKE™ Zones 5-9

This dwarf, thornless raspberry is part of the Brazel-Berries® line of small fruit-bearing plants and deserves an invitation to a small-space cocktail party. The canes grow between two and three feet tall. Keep these party guests happy by removing those stems that bore fruit in the past season in the fall. Leave the canes that didn't flower and produce fruit, because they will produce berries the following summer. The berries on these shorter plants are just as large and tasty as those produced by larger raspberry bushes.

'PATIO SNACKER' CUCUMBER

This short, branched plant is perfect for containers and small trellises. It's no wonder that Burpee Home Gardens calls this "a cucumber vending machine." Make this green hour guest comfortable by providing a trellis or obelisk that is three to four feet high. A good host will also supply fertilizer and water regularly.

'SWEET HEAT' PEPPERS

As long as you have a location that receives at least six hours of direct sun, you can invite these mildly spicy peppers to your container garden. The plants grow to about a foot high and wide and produce peppers that are about four inches long. Grow one plant per pot, using a container that's at least a foot in diameter. If you grow several of these in decorative containers, they'll be hot party decorations as well as spicy edibles.

'HONEY NUT' SQUASH

Renee's Garden Seeds originally sent these baby butternut squash to my garden party, and they quickly became one of my must-have vegetables. The vines are shorter and can be grown up a small trellis or left to trail out of a container without consuming the entire patio. The squash themselves are also small. When cooked, they are perfect for two to four people. Best of all, the squash are sweet and flavorful.

Garden Produce Cocktails

Just about any fruit and vegetable can be used during the cocktail hour.
Here are just a few suggestions for bringing your garden into your evening green hour refreshments.

- MUDDLE IT UP. In cocktails, the word *muddle* means to crush, smash and otherwise mix an ingredient so that the flavors are released into the liquid. You can place berries, greens, herbs or vegetables into the bottom of a mason jar or cocktail shaker and mash them with a wooden spoon or cocktail muddler tool. Most of the time, the solids are strained out before the drink is poured and served.

- BLEND AND STRAIN. If you have a juicer, by all means experiment with tossing beets, carrots, peas or any other garden bounty into the machine and adding an ounce or two of fresh juice into your evening beverage. Those who don't have a juicer can extract veggie juices by placing the produce in a food processor or blender. If necessary, add a bit of water or other liquid and blend until you have a smooth puree. Drape a clean dishtowel into a bowl and pour the puree onto the cloth. (Be prepared for stains. Even green veggies will permanently mark the cloth.) Once all the puree is in the cloth, gather the sides of the towel up and twist so that the juice comes out into the bowl, leaving the pulp inside.

- TURN UP THE HEAT. Hot pepper infused tequila has become fairly standard, but you can add some fire to just about any liquid. Take two or three organically grown hot peppers and coarsely chop them, seeds and all. Place them in a glass measuring cup or bowl, add the spirit or juice of your choice and let sit for at least two hours. Strain out the solids and pour the amped-up beverage back into the bottle.

- GARNISH. Fresh berries and citrus slices are common garnishes for drinks, but most veggies can work well too. Some favorites include pickled green beans or Brussels sprouts, radishes, carrot sticks, sugar snap peas, cucumbers, cherry tomatoes and matchstick summer squash. The idea behind a garnish is to provide visual appeal, fragrance and taste, so consider all aspects of a fruit or vegetable before plunking it in your beverage. Cabbage, for example, might not be the best choice...

If you're going to make your vegetable garden into a space for green hour celebrations, you'll want them to be both functional and attractive. Fortunately, these aren't mutually exclusive. There are so many vegetables that are both tasty and beautiful that it's almost impossible not to grow a beautiful vegetable garden. Here are some of those tasty and beautiful vegetables. These are also varieties that either can be harvested over a long period of time or can be re-sown through the summer so that the cocktail hour garden is never bare.

MULTI-COLORED LETTUCE *(Lactuca sativa)*

There are so many varieties of lettuce that have interesting colors and textures that it's impossible to grow them all. Invite as many as you can to your green hour by sowing seeds. It never ceases to amaze me that people buy lettuce in six-packs when for the same amount of money they could have fifty or more plants instead of only a half dozen!

Lettuce is easy to grow from seed: just sprinkle it on the surface of the soil, lightly press it in with your hand so that the seeds make good contact with the ground and keep moist while the seeds germinate. If you plant the seeds close together, you can pluck up young plants and eat those in salads while waiting for others to form larger heads. Cut the oldest leaves only to extend the life of each lettuce plant, but once they start to elongate and flower (also called bolting) pull the entire plant for salad and start again.

In areas where summer temperatures are very hot, grow most of your lettuce in the winter, spring and fall. More temperate regions can sow lettuce seeds every three to four weeks from spring through the summer for continual harvest.

With leaves that are this lovely, there's no reason not to plant lettuce in window boxes, flower beds or patio pots. Sow seeds in empty spaces in the spring and eat the salad greens as surrounding plants grow.

RAINBOW CHARD
(Beta vulgaris subsp. vulgaris)

Chard is not only ornamental, it's delicious and one of the most versatile vegetables you can cook with. Use chard in any spinach recipe, harvest large leaves to make assorted "wraps" or use it in place of pasta in lasagna recipes. Can you tell I'm a fan of this plant?

Grow chard from seed that's sown about three to six inches apart and covered lightly with soil. Harvest by cutting the oldest leaves so that the plant will continue to produce new foliage into the cold season. Chard is also quite frost tolerant, so the plants you start early in the season can still be producing into autumn.

TUSCAN KALE (Brassica oleracea var. acephala)

Another must-have guest at your veggie green hour is Tuscan kale. This plant is extremely ornamental and becomes even more so as it ages. Also called dinosaur kale (a good name for this vegetable if you want to get small children interested in tasting something green), this variety can be eaten raw or cooked. Tuscan kale has a very sweet flavor and will grow quite tall as long as you harvest the oldest leaves but not the newest growth. It will sail through light frost and, in some parts of the country, will continue to produce well after you've moved your cocktail hour into warmer surroundings.

BEETS (Beta vulgaris)

There aren't many plants that can say their roots are as delicious as their leaves, but beets are one of them. They can be pulled from the soil when small or left to grow large, and they'll be equally delicious and sweet. Like chard, these veggies will light up with the rays of the setting sun, so if you have a location that is illuminated during sunset, be sure to plant beets where they can shine in a green hour spotlight.

RED NOODLE BEANS (Vigna unguiculata)

These aren't really beans but a form of cowpea. You'll need a trellis, tall obelisk or other support to grow them, but they are so prolific and delicious that it's worth providing them with something to grow on.

The long, red beans grow in pairs, and once they start to form you can almost watch them grow! This is a vegetable that gives ornamental annual vines a run for their money... once you invite  the red noodle bean to your cocktail party, you might not want to invite the morning glory again. An added bonus is that unlike purple beans, these keep most of their color when cooked! The young pods are also flexible, tempting creative cooks into experimenting with edible wrap ties and knots.

Whether growing vegetables in containers or in the ground, use the same design principles you would for making any garden visually appealing. First and foremost, put the plants where they will thrive. The right plant in the right place will be healthier and therefore more attractive.

Secondly, group plants together in clusters of odd numbers, using greater numbers of smaller plants and fewer larger ones. Three pots filled with five chard plants each will make a stronger visual statement than one chard plant in one pot. In fact, one charming way to display a potted veggie garden is by lining the pots into rows, with the shorter plants in front of the medium to tall varieties. For example, place five pots of chard, in front of five pots of broccoli, in front of five pots of tomatoes, to create a small garden.

Additionally, think about alternating colors and textures of foliage. Plant vegetables you enjoy eating, by all means, but grow or arrange them according to leaf size and color. For instance, place green-foliaged plants with the blue-green Tuscan kale or the red-stemmed chard. Place plants with very large leaves, such as summer squash, behind a border of fine leaves, such as curly parsley.

Once we begin to see vegetables as ornamental annuals in addition to being edible, there are no limits to the ways we can plan the green hour garden.

Nasturtiums, chard and parsley can be used as ingredients in cocktails, as ingredients for hors d'oeuvres or for garnishes that are edible. When eaten raw, all of these are best-picked when the leaves are young and tender.

Party Planning:

- Although you can regularly find seed for sale online, local garden centers may run out by mid-summer. If there are veggies that you know you'll replant, buy enough seed early in the summer for successive sowings.

- As soon as one crop finishes, plant something else. When the first sowing of radishes, peas, lettuce and other cool weather crops is finished, it opens up valuable space for mid-summer or fall planting. Plant varieties of vegetables that mature in three months or less in the empty spaces. Carrots, lettuce, pak choi (bok choy), radishes and broccoli rabe are perfect for mid-season planting.

- In small spaces, you can underplant tall plants such as broccoli or eggplant with shorter, fast crops such as lettuce. Be sure that your soil is well-amended for such intensive growing. Applying compost and digging it in (for those who till) or layering it on top (for the no-till folks) annually, along with a general organic fertilizer, will ensure that you have soil that's rich enough to support concentrated planting.

- Don't worry about crop rotation. Most home gardens are too small to vary a planting scheme too much, and moving a tomato or squash a mere ten to fifteen feet away does little to prevent diseases. In limited spaces, just keep soils amended with organic matter and fertilizer. It's also wise to apply a layer of mulch for moisture conservation, disease suppression and further enrichment.

You are invited

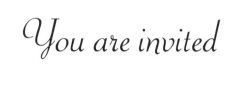

TO:

Homegrown Refreshments

WHERE:

In Your Yard & Garden

WHEN:

5 to 8 P.M.

RSVP:

To Herbs, Fruits and Edible Flowers

Nine

Herbs, Flowers and Other Beverage Ingredients

Have you heard the saying, "The little things are the big things"? In the garden, as in life, this adage has a great deal of merit. I left the little things for the end of this book for several reasons, but not because they are minor players in the garden. Far from it.

First of all, it makes sense to start with the overall picture, and to build any garden by starting with the layout and larger plants. All landscapes and garden designs begin with what we have and are created from there. After the large-scale work is done, focus can turn to smaller plants and ornaments.

Yet, it's important to remember that when we look at our daily experience with the garden, it's often those small moments of beauty or wonder that create our most pleasurable moments. Additionally, all aspects of the cocktail hour garden come together with the tiny sprigs of herbs, flowers and other ingredients and garnishes. Touch, sight, scent and taste all combine in the plants we grow for culinary purposes. These herbs, berries and flowers supply the small touches that lift our spirits, make us smile and turn something routine or ordinary into a sensual *experience*.

All the flowers and foliage in this arrangement are edible as well as pretty. You may recognize the marigolds, lavender, summer Phlox and nasturtium flowers. Lesser-known edible blooms in this mix include Agastache, mint and oregano flowers.

These plants provide opportunities to be creative in the garden as well as in the kitchen. As I began thinking about this chapter, I decided to get into the herb and flower mood by walking through my gardens. Soon, I was picking stems from some of the many blooms and foliage that are edible. Moving from the flowerbeds to my herb and vegetable gardens, I quickly had more stems than I could hold. The resulting arrangement held only a fraction of the herbs and edible flowers available to me in the garden on that one day. It was a clear demonstration of the wealth of plants we can grow that are beautiful and appetizing.

The beauty of growing herbs, edible flowers and fruit is that many of them bring more to the party than a flavor or use as a pretty garnish. Whether it's fragrance, bright colors or value as a reliable garden plant, most of these plants deserve an invitation to many of your garden celebrations even before you start preparing snacks or beverages.

Herbs

Not including old slang for marijuana, there are two ways to define the term *herb*. For most people, this word refers to plants that are useful for medicines, food and flavoring. Some include perfume in this group, and cooks distinguish herbs – the leafy part of a plant – from spices, which are made from all other parts such as bark, roots, berries, seeds and stamens. In the study of botany, however, an herb is any plant that dies to the ground instead of growing from a woody stem. So to a botanist, most perennials and annuals are herbaceous and could be described as herbs.

In the green hour garden, an herb is any plant that is useful for enhancing our evening relaxation experience, with emphasis on the edible and thoroughly enjoyable. There are, after all, many plants that *could* be eaten if sustaining life without poisoning was the only criterion. For the cocktail hour, however, a pleasurable taste and fragrance are essential.

Old shipping crates are turned into an herb garden at Cassis Monna & Filles on the beautiful Ile d'Orleans in Quebec. This use of recycled lumber can inspire contained and raised beds for your cocktail hour garden.

Garden Tea

There are many ways herbs can be used for beverages. We can use them to make tea, either hot or iced. My favorite way to brew iced tea from fresh herbs is to place the newly picked leaves in a glass jar or pitcher, fill with water, cover the top and place this in the sun for between two to four hours. This "sun tea" can also be made using standard tea bags, but for fresh herbs, this method is especially effective. Sun-heated water becomes hot enough to transfer flavors but doesn't rise to boiling temperatures, so it doesn't cook the foliage.

Tea-based beverages have become increasingly popular. These can be made with or without alcohol (am I the only one who dislikes the term mocktail?), so the tea that you brew in the sun can make an easy transition from afternoon to evening beverage. Iced tea becomes perfect for the cocktail hour with the squeeze of a citrus, a touch of sweetening, sprigs of herbs for garnish and the addition of a spirit, if you so choose.

Although traditional teas such as black, green or mint can be used, don't be afraid to try unconventional herbs. Add basil to lemon grass in your pitcher, or make a tea using sage. Experimenting is more than half the fun...it's the entire point of growing some of these plants. After letting the herbs sit in the sun, chill the mix first and then strain and taste before adding any other ingredients. The worst that can happen is that you don't like what you've brewed and you use the liquid to water your potted plants.

Herbs don't have to be brewed into tea before using them in beverages, of course:

- Flavorful foliage can be crushed (muddled) alone or with sugar, citrus or other ingredients before being added to a pitcher or cocktail shaker.

- You can put herbs in with liquids in a blender or food processor, blending until the leaves are finely chopped but not necessarily pureed so much that the drink becomes too thick. Most of the time, the bits of stem and foliage are strained out of the beverage before serving.

- Flavor can be transferred by making a simple syrup and tossing in the herbs of choice once the syrup has simmered and been taken off the stove. Chop herbs coarsely, add to the pot after the sugar has dissolved and let it sit off the heat while the syrup cools. Strain out the solids and store the flavored syrup in a mason jar in the refrigerator. Such syrups usually keep for at least a week.

GARNISH AWAY! Finally, of course, herbs are the perfect garnish. A sprig of mint, lemon verbena or basil makes any drink more pleasurable visually, and the fragrance from the herbs is inhaled as you bring the glass to your lips. Tall stems such as lovage, lavender and lemon grass can be garnishes or swizzle sticks, adding flavor and scent along with a dash of drama. And don't forget to adorn the pitcher or punch bowl when making drinks for a crowd. Herbs will be looking lovely in the carafe, adding their flavor until the guests are ready for refills.

A Toast To...
Simple Syrups

A simple syrup is true to its name. The classic recipe is a straightforward combination of equal parts of sugar and water. A common recommendation is to put one cup of water and one cup of sugar in a saucepan and bring to a simmer until the sugar is dissolved.

Because the sugar is fairly concentrated, only a small amount is used per drink.

HONEY OR MAPLE SYRUP
Those who avoid refined sugar can make a similar mix of honey or maple syrup and water, knowing that they each add their distinctive flavors to the end beverage. Because each is already a liquid, slightly less water should be used.

STEVIA
Stevia, a sweetener made from the herb *Stevia rebaudiana*, can be used in a simple syrup for those who want to avoid all sugars. Because it is far sweeter than sugar, you'd use 1/8 cup of stevia powder (available at natural food stores) to one cup of water. Be sure to read labels on store-bought stevias; some of these have assorted additives along with the sweetener.

Do you grow stevia? You can make the simple syrup by putting a cup of chopped stevia stems in a jar with a cup of water. Refrigerate the mix and strain after 24 to 48 hours, then bring to a simmer before storing in the refrigerator again. Note that the flavor is not improved by steeping longer, and in fact can become bitter with longer steeping or cooking the foliage in the liquid.

OTHER FLAVORINGS
Beyond adding the herbs of your choice, simple syrups can be flavored with spices, citrus peel or other fruits. Whole peels or fruit can be left in the syrup for a day or two, but if storing for up to a week or 10 days, let the flavors infuse in the cooling syrup, strain and refrigerate. When storing a jar of simple syrup, be sure to label it with the date it was made and the flavorings used.

AGAVE NECTAR
Want to avoid simple syrup all together? Many people are now choosing agave nectar for sweeting everything from iced tea to cocktails. Like stevia, agave nectar is sweeter than sugar, so less is needed. It's also low on the glycemic index although high in fructose, so a little goes a long way.

Herbs for the Cocktail Hour Garden

When a good host or hostess introduces guests to each other at an evening gathering, he or she will often mention something interesting about each person to get the conversation flowing. It is my great pleasure to reacquaint you with the following herbs, and in order to keep *this* party flowing, I'll mention some tidbits about these plants that you might not be familiar with.

BASIL *(Ocimum basilicum)* Zones 10b-11

I know you've met basil before, most likely as an annual that's especially important for Italian cooking and seasoning tomato dishes. Basil is often called

one of the "sweet herbs." It's been popular in North America since the 1600s. In case you thought that being pesto and spaghetti's BFF was its only claim to fame, however, know that members of the genus *Ocimum* have been used worldwide in religious rituals and in many cultures as a symbol of love, attraction and good fortune. According to the Herb Society of America, basil has also had cameo appearances in the works of Shakespeare and in poems by Percy Bysshe Shelley, John Keats and Edna St. Vincent Millay.

In your green hour garden, you'll probably want to invite the sweet Italian basil, lemon basil, spicy bush basil and African blue basil, among others. Each has its own distinctive take on the basil fragrance and taste, but in order to grow, all want warm temperatures and at least six hours of direct sun.

Just between us, I've *heard* that in Colonial times women would make two bunches of basil as they bustled about the kitchen. One would be for the cooking pot and the other to tuck between their breasts so the fragrance would waft up as they worked...or otherwise.

BAY *(Laurus nobilis)* Zones 8-10

If you live where this shrub survives outdoors, you'll want it as a permanent plant at your garden party, but in colder climates, do invite bay to stay in a large container and be your houseguest over the wintertime. *Laurus nobilis* is filled with phytochemicals and has a long history of being studied and used medicinally. But, it's mainly bay's role as a culinary herb that brings this laurel to our frequent attention. We're all familiar with how nicely bay mingles with soups and casseroles, but it's also quite delightful when steeped with the liquids used in chocolate recipes and cocktails. Yes, chocolate; this herb can be with you from the green hour straight through dessert.

CILANTRO *(Coriandrum sativum)*
Annual in all zones

Whether you call this guest cilantro or coriander, know that this herb has traveled the world and is equally at home in the cuisines of many cultures. It has also been used in a tea for digestive disorders. Know that cilantro often leaves the party early... it tends to bolt (go to seed) when the weather gets hot. There are those who love this herb so much that they sow seeds every two to three weeks through the summer so that there are always new plants in the garden. There are other people, however, who think cilantro tastes like soap. Needless to say, if you're in that last group, you don't have to issue repeat invitations.

DILL *(Anethum graveolens)* Annual in all zones

This herb is best known, perhaps, for being part of that famous duo of Dill and Pickle. But once you get to know this plant (shown above), you'll understand that it is equally at home in a crowd with potatoes, eggs, salads and curry dishes, not to mention bouquets of flowers. In the cocktail hour garden, dill can be used in beverages or as a garnish. The flower umbels make perfect natural umbrella-shaped garnishes for drinks in tall glasses. Dill fits right in with cucumber and lime in beverages and salads. In the garden, it mixes well with perennials, shrubs or other annuals because it doesn't take up much space. Note that dill does self-seed, so if you're not a fan of annuals that will crash the party for years to come, be sure to cut the flowers off before they set seeds.

LAVENDER (*Lavandula* spp.) Zones 5-10 depending on variety

In Chapter 2, we celebrated lavender as a fragrant herb, but since this sub-shrub has been cultivated since the Middle Ages, it's clearly a plant that's seen a thing or two. Lavender has been bathed in, eaten, smoked and used for healing, internally and externally. It's been applied to cloth, furniture and stinky feet alike. Lavender has been used to repel fleas, treat head lice and improve moods...I guess it makes sense that a plant promising to suppress lice and fleas would also lighten your disposition.

Lavender blends well with citrus flavors, blueberries, vanilla and gin. Think lavender lemonade, a blueberry-lavender fizz or a Meyer lemon and lavender Tom Collins.

LEMON BALM (*Melissa officinalis*) Zones 3-9

Lemon balm may not be the best-dressed herb at your party, but you might want to send it an invitation anyway. Although this herb is in the mint family, it's not as well known as its rambunctious cousins. Early North American colonists used *Melissa officinalis* to attract honeybees and as a lemon substitute for flavoring tea and jellies. It's species name, *officinalis*, means "used in medicine," and famous herbalist John Gerard wrote that "Bawme [balm] drunken in wine is good against the bitings of venomous beasts, comforts the heart and driveth away all melancholy and sadness."

One type of unhappiness this plant is sure to cure is the sorrow felt by people with black and brown thumbs. Like other mints, this is one of the easiest herbs to grow. In fact, those with small gardens might want to confine this to a pot so that they don't end up fighting it as it spreads. It's common for lemon balm to brown out a bit as the season goes on, so place it in the back of the garden where it won't call attention to itself.

Use this herb as an ingredient or garnish in any lemon-based drink, or mix it with other mints for a refreshing citrus flavor.

LEMON GRASS (*Cymbopogon citratus*) Zones 9-10

Unfortunately, people have come to associate lemon grass with a scent used in spa candles and soaps, not a real herb. Of course you know that in Thai cuisine this is a must-grow plant for flavoring, but did you know that it's a member of the sugar cane family? One of the traditional medicinal plants in several countries, this grass is also just plain attractive in the garden or in a pot. Use it to flavor liquids, muddle it in a glass or chop the interior, tender parts for cooking. But here's another idea: how about using the stems for swizzle sticks?

LEMON VERBENA (*Aloysia triphylla*) Zones 8-10

This herb could have invented the entire concept of aromatherapy. Rubbing and inhaling a few fresh leaves makes everyone instantly feel better. In the garden center, when I've handed a sprig to a customer who was unfamiliar with the herb, there hasn't been

Lemon grass stalks make the perfect swizzle sticks for tall beverages. Clip off a sturdy stem and remove the lower leaves. The remaining leaves on the top can be knotted or tied in a bow, clipping away the excess so that the finished stick is 8 to 12 inches tall.

a single time when the client hasn't first smiled and then purchased a plant. A spring of crushed lemon verbena instantly makes tea, sparkling water, wine, beer or any mixed drink more interesting and delicious. We value this plant so much at my house that we bring one inside for the winter, picking sprigs as long as the foliage holds up indoors. And we always have at least two plants growing in the cocktail hour garden, so there's an abundance of mood-altering foliage.

LOVAGE *(Levisticum officinale)* Zones 3-8

By no means a subtle herb, but with a name like lovage, why should it beat around the bush? Although this plant claims love in its name, it wasn't named for the emotion but for its likeness to another herb. "Lovage" is derived from "love-ache," but "ache" was a medieval name for parsley. Nevertheless, those who have forgotten to buy celery for Bloody Mary garnishing will be glad if they have lovage in the garden, since the flavors are so similar. In fact, you may love lovage so much that you might never purchase celery again.

MINT *(Menthe* spp.) Zones 3-8 depending on variety

You know how to use mint in your beverages. What you may not know is that this herb is a classic example of everyone blaming the mistress. You see, in Greek mythology, Menthe (aka Mintha) was a nymph who was having an affair with Hades, the god of the Underworld. Needless to say, when Hades' wife Persephone stumbled upon them one day, she wasn't happy. And like many wives before and after her, she blamed the mistress, not her husband. To punish Menthe, she turned her into a plant that would spread into pathways so that people would step on her forever. Hades decided that it might be of some comfort to Menthe to have a pleasing scent, so that everyone would *smile* when they walked all over her. Or crushed her to make a mojito. Since it didn't seem to occur to Hades that Menthe might have preferred being returned to nymph form, the least we can do is raise our glasses to this herb/sprite. *Menthe* has found a way to vigorously persist in gardens, beverages and flavorings around the world, so perhaps she has triumphed in the end.

Mint is one of the party guests that knows no boundaries. If your garden is small, keep mints in a pot and even grow them as annuals. There's a reason that this pot isn't placed on the ground: mint will root where the stems touch soil, and it will grow down through a drainage hole to invade the soil below. If you don't want mint in your gardens but appreciate it in your drinks, keep the pots on hard surfaces.

PARSLEY *(Petroselinum crispum)*
Zones 5-11 biennial

You're probably bored with parsley, and who can blame you? It's the most widely used herb in North America. You know that it comes with curly or flat leaves and is often used as a garnish, left on the plate and discarded. It's reported that parsley freshens the breath, but then why is mouthwash still so popular? In any case, it's clearly going to take something compelling to get parsley trending again.

So how about this: the Green Lantern Cocktail. A delightful, cooling drink that will put the green in any green hour, whether it's made with alcohol or not. Here's how it's done for four tall drinks.

Green Lantern Cocktail

Puree the following ingredients in a blender or food processor:

> 1 packed cup parsley leaves
> Zest of one lime, finely grated
> 1 cup cold water
> ½ cup fresh lime juice
> 3 tablespoons agave nectar or honey

Once these are well-blended, strain through a fine sieve. Divide into four tall glasses and add ice. Fill the glass with sparkling mineral water and garnish with a sprig of parsley and a lime wedge. You can also add 2 ounces of the spirit of your choice – vodka, gin or jalapeno-infused tequila work especially well.

Note that there are other cocktails that have been called a Green Lantern. To avoid confusion, perhaps we should rename this one The Garnish's Revenge.

Pineapple sage is one of the aromatherapy plants; just a sniff makes you feel better! The combination of the African blue basil on the left and the 'Golden Delicious' pineapple sage on the right works especially well, because they are similar in height all summer long. Like the green-leaf pineapple sage *(Salvia elegans)*, 'Golden Delicious' produces red flowers in the very late fall.

PINEAPPLE SAGE *(Salvia elegans)* Zones 8-10

This plant is a shrub where hardy, but in most of North America it's grown as an annual. This herb is traditionally prized as a remedy for anxiety and depression, and whether it's really medicinal or not, the fragrance and bright red flowers do tend to cheer people up. In fact, the Internet abounds with posts from those who are merrily mixing up pineapple sage daiquiris, mojitos and margaritas. This herb is being tucked into ice tea and sparkling water or combined with grapefruit juice and club soda for a refreshing cooler. The yellow-leaf variety, 'Golden Delicious', will add liveliness to your garden as well as your glass, making it a must-plant herb for sunny gardens.

ROSEMARY (*Rosmarinus officinalis*)

It's said that consuming rosemary increases the flow of blood to the brain, thereby enhancing memory. I eat a lot of rosemary, so why can't I remember where I left my cell phone? Traditional medicinal uses and my own forgetfulness aside, this highly aromatic herb makes a very refreshing addition to all sorts of beverages. From lemonade to iced tea and white wine spritzers, a small sprig of rosemary will jazz up many drinks.

Rosemary is evergreen in warm climates, and those in cold areas can bring the plant indoors in a pot for the winter. The secret to overwintering success is a sunny window and regular watering. When growing this plant indoors, herbalists have a saying: "A dry rosemary is a dead rosemary." Also, look for the variety called 'Salem', as it seems to be more tolerant of being inside and winter's reduced hours of daylight.

SAGE (*Salvia officinalis*) Zones 4-8 depending on variety

Because of its anti-bacterial, anti-fungal and anti-inflammatory properties, sage has been used medicinally for at least two thousand years. Because of its ability to ward off bacteria, it was employed in ancient Greece and Rome as a preservative for meats, and many cultures have used it to treat skin conditions.

In beverages, the flavor of fresh sage pairs very well with fresh orange juice. Muddle some sage leaves, shake with orange juice and strain into a glass, adding sparkling water and garnishing with a sage leaf and a twist of orange peel. This is refreshing "as is" for all ages, or the spirit of your choice can be added for adults.

SCENTED GERANIUMS (*Pelargonium* hybrids) Zones 10-11

I'd venture to guess that there are as many fragrant *Pelargoniums* as there are scented candles. From rose to lime, cinnamon and apricot, you'll find a scented geranium that mimics most spices and fruits. There are dozens of mint, citrus and rose varieties. I've even read of these plants having an oak fragrance (go figure) and some that are simply described as "pungent."

The leaves from these plants have been used to flavor jelly, sorbet and other sweet concoctions for decades, so the leap to adding them to simple syrup for cocktails a natural one. It doesn't make much sense to use the citrus scents if you have the real lemon, lime or orange in the house, but being able to craft a rose-flavored cocktail from a garden where there are no roses has a certain appeal. *Pelargoniums* are also one of the easiest plants to grow, since they are fairly forgiving about dry soil and being root bound.

One of the simplest and most sophisticated garnishes is a sprig of fresh thyme. Use a single stem per glass or plate.

STEVIA (*Stevia rebaudiana*)
Zones 9-10

If you've broken up with sugar, stevia might just become your new BFF. It's not the most ornamental of plants, but people still want it at their garden party because "Stevia is just so *sweet*." It grows well in soils with good drainage, so put it in a pot if you have moist gardens or clay. When you plant stevia in a container, for heaven's sake, don't cover up the drainage hole. Know too that like many *really* sweet people, stevia is often best in small doses and can't stay sugary under pressure; less is often more, and high heat or long storage can make stevia drinks and syrups bitter.

THYME (*Thymus* spp. and hybrids)
Zones 2-9 depending on variety

The ancient Greeks associated thyme with style and elegance, the Romans with courage, and the French with really great food. In the cocktail hour garden, it might be your go-to plant for a simple but sophisticated garnish. Be it on a plate or in a beverage, thyme marries well with citrus. Combine thyme-infused simple syrup with grapefruit, lemon or lime when you want to feel stylish, elegant and courageous.

Just For Fun...
Garnish On Ice

Some years ago, a dear friend of mine was on a very strict diet that limited her food choices. Knowing that she was going to join us for Thanksgiving that year, I went out into garden before hard frost and picked all the edible flowers that I could find. I poked these into ice cube trays filled with water, the small flowers whole and single petals from the large ones. These trays were squirrelled away until the third Thursday in November, so that the sparkling water that my friend was drinking could have a special, holiday appeal.

We don't have to wait for such circumstances to enjoy ice-encapsulated blooms. Frozen flowers and herbs make a special garnish in green hour beverages, be they mineral water, white wine coolers or intricately mixed cocktails. Although these ice cubes are for garnish, not flavoring, be sure to use flowers and leaves that are edible and organically grown.

Edible Flowers

Not all flowers are edible, so don't start to graze in your cocktail hour garden indiscriminately. Also, be sure that you have a plant accurately identified before eating the blooms. Since some common names are applied to several completely different plants, make sure that the flower that's popped into a drink or onto a plate is truly the edible variety. This is one reason being familiar with botanical names is of value.

It's also important to recognize that just because a flower can be eaten doesn't mean it's delicious. There are flowers that aren't poisonous, certainly, but they also aren't very tasty. Many people think that the strong flavor of the marigold falls into the "I wouldn't want to eat a lot of it" category. And just like foods, there are also flowers that some people might have a reaction to, especially when consumed in large quantities – so eat new flowers with moderation. Finally, flowers that you eat or add to beverages should have been organically grown.

These cautions aside, flowers can be an attractive way to add color and flavor to your green hour. Here is a list of plants that are not only ornamental in the garden but are edible as well. Note that the flowers of all the herbs listed earlier in this chapter are also edible, so they're not repeated here.

- **Anise or hummingbird mints** (*Agastache* spp. and hybrids) are licorice flavored and slightly sweet.

- **Bee balm** (*Monarda didyma*) is a bit minty, and the petals can also have a citrus and sweet flavor. Frankly, these smell very much like Fruit Loops cereal.

- **Borage** (*Borago officinalis*) tastes like cucumber, but since parts of the plant are furry and the herb often has a diuretic effect, it should be used in moderation.

Lovely hibiscus has a mild citrus flavor.

- **Calendula** (*Calendula officinalis*) is peppery and slightly bitter.
- **Chrysanthemum** (*Dendranthema* hybrids) flowers are mild, but the base of the petals can be bitter.
- **Dianthus, aka pinks,** (*Dianthus* sp.) are spicy and can be sweet, but with too many petals, there is a bitter undertone.
- **Hibiscus, aka tropical hibiscus,** (*Hibiscus rosa-sinensis*) has a mild citrus flavor.
- **Lilac** (*Syringa vulgaris*) has a mild (surprise!) lilac flavor.
- **Marigold** (*Tagetes* spp. and hybrids) can be bitter and should never be eaten in large amounts. 'Lemon Gem' is said to have the best flavor.
- **Nasturtium** (*Tropaeolum majus*) is spicy and peppery, with a dash of sweetness in the flower spur.
- **Pansy** (*Viola* x *wittrockiana*) is very mild but can have a sweet, wintergreen flavor.
- **Purslane** (*Portulaca* hybrids) is sweet and tart at the same time. Note that these flowers close up in the evening.
- **Rose** (*Rosa* spp. and hybrids) varies in flavor depending on variety and where it is raised. It is said that the darker the rose, the more flavorful the flower.
- **Tulip** (*Tulipa* spp. and hybrids) petals have a fresh cucumber or salad green flavor.

Not many people realize that tulip petals are edible. Tuliptinis, anyone?

Berries

While garden-grown berries are delicious and beautiful, instead of putting these in the cocktail hour garden, consider placing them elsewhere on the property. It's not that berry plants aren't ornamental, because many of them are quite attractive. But the practicalities of growing these plants preclude them from being completely suitable in the green hour garden.

First of all, most fruit trees and bushes require several plants in order to have much of a crop to harvest. Blueberries and quince, for example, have more fruit when there are several shrubs near each other to ensure good cross-pollination. Most apple trees require more than one plant for fertilization, and because each raspberry cane doesn't hold that many ripe berries at any one time, having a few rows of these plants produces the best yields.

And then there is the issue of the birds and other wildlife. Many a gardener optimistically plants a blueberry or other fruiting plant, only to find that the majority of the produce is carried away before humans can get it picked. People who are serious about growing berries get a good quality bird netting that can be pinned securely to the ground.

So perhaps it's best to confine the growing of berry plants to areas behind or beyond the cocktail hour garden. This doesn't prevent you from occasionally taking your evening green hour into those gardens, however, and toasting the berry plants and the netting that makes your harvest possible.

Growing fruit in pots is another matter, however. It is fun to grow some of the shorter varieties of berry bushes in a container so that when the berries are ripe, you have them at hand for munching or tossing in a glass. Before and after the harvest, the pots can be growing elsewhere on the property. Just be sure to move the pots into your cocktail hour garden before the birds get the fruit, and tie some netting or tulle around the plants and pots to protect your harvest.

Raspberries are the perfect plants for garnishes, drink ingredients or snacking. Whether they're invited to your cocktail party as garden or container plants, be sure to cut down the canes that bore fruit at the end of the season. Leave those stems that grew but didn't produce fruit, because those will be studded with tasty berries the next season.

Herb, Flower and Berry Cocktails

Basil Margarita

For each drink:
5 or 6 large basil leaves (or three
  sprigs of lime or spice varieties)
1 oz. fresh lime juice
1 oz. agave nectar
2 oz. blue agave tequila
Lime and basil for garnish
Salt for rim (optional)

If you want salt on the rim of your glass, rub it with a lime wedge first and press the salt against the edge. Muddle the basil a bit in a mason jar or cocktail shaker, add the lime juice and agave nectar and muddle again. Add the tequila and ice cubes, and shake well. Strain into the glass and garnish with the basil and lime.

Nasturtium Cocktail

For each drink:
6 to 8 nasturtium flowers
1½ oz. fresh lime or grapefruit juice
1 oz. simple syrup or agave nectar
2 oz. vodka
A pinch of freshly ground black pepper
Ice
A nasturtium leaf for garnish

This cocktail celebrates the peppery nature of the nasturtium foliage and flower. Muddle the flowers in a cocktail shaker or mason jar. Add the simple syrup

and citrus juice and muddle again. Add the vodka, pinch of pepper and four ice cubes, and shake vigorously. Strain into the glass of your choice and garnish with a small nasturtium leaf, floating it lily pad-style. This drink can be poured into a tall glass over ice and topped with sparkling mineral water for a refreshing cooler.

Cucumber Herb Cooler

For each drink:
½ organically-grown cucumber (about ¾ cup
  that's been chopped, skin and all)
Three sprigs each of dill, basil, parsley, and
  coriander (about 2 tablespoons of each herb)
½ oz. fresh lemon juice
½ oz. honey or agave nectar
½ cup water
Sparkling mineral water
Edible flower petals for garnish
Optional: 1 ½ oz. gin

Place the cucumber, herbs, lemon juice and honey in a food processor or blender with the water. Blend until well mixed but not totally pureed, then pour through a fine sieve into a bowl or glass measuring cup. Press lightly with a large spoon to get most of the liquid. Discard the solids and pour the herb mix over ice in a tall glass. Top with sparkling water and garnish with an edible flower. (If you want to make an alcoholic beverage, add the gin before topping off with the sparkling water.)

Fresh Blueberry Cocktail

For each drink:
2 oz. vodka
1 oz. lemon juice
½ oz. agave nectar
10 fresh blueberries plus
   one for garnish
Ice
Two sprigs of fresh mint

Muddle the blueberries in a mason jar with one sprig of the mint. Add the lemon juice, vodka, agave nectar and three ice cubes and shake vigorously. Strain into a cocktail glass and garnish with one whole blueberry and a sprig of mint. This is a tart version of the drink; those who prefer a sweeter beverage can double the amount of agave nectar.

Party Planning

- Most herbs grow best in full sun and well-drained soils. They are frequently more flavorful when grown on the lean side as well, so an herb garden isn't the space where lots of fertilizer and organic matter are needed. Plant in soil that is just fertile enough to promote growth and water longer but less often to encourage deep root systems.

- Herbs that will be overwintered indoors should be raised in pots that are large enough to accommodate their growth. When a plant is in too small a container, the top growth will be limited, and it's more difficult to keep the plant well-hydrated over the winter season.

- Bay trees do just fine with lower levels of light in the winter, but when grown inside warm houses are much more prone to scale. Those who have a window in an unheated garage that doesn't go below freezing during the winter can very successfully keep a bay there, preventing scale infestations. Water the plant every two or three weeks when the soil feels dry, but refrain from fertilizing until the bay tree goes outside again in the spring.

- Clipping off spent flowers often stimulates the production of new blooms. Consider using the petals from edible flowers that are just going by as garnish on food or in drinks. You'll benefit from having your plants dead-headed and your cocktail hour will be more colorful for it.

Inverted clay pots make good stands for elevating bowl planters. In this grouping, they put the herbs right at easy picking height. Herbs in these planters include (left to right) sage, lemon verbena, lavender, silver-edged thyme, stevia, Alaska nasturtiums, bronze fennel and lemon thyme.

Index

Index

Index

Resources

Those interested in the cocktail hour might appreciate the following books as much as I have:

100 Years of Cocktails, by H.L. Holbough, Amazon Kindle Edition, 2012

The Book of Absinthe: A Cultural History, by Phil Baker, Grove Press, 2003

Cocktails: A Global History, by Joseph M. Carlin, Reaktion Books, 2012

The Drunken Botanist: the Plants that Create the World's Great Drinks, by Amy Stewart, Algonquin Books, 2013

Edible Cocktails: From Garden to Glass – Seasonal Cocktails with a Fresh Twist, by Natalie Bovis, Adams Media, 2012

A History of the World in 6 Glasses, by Tom Standage, Walker Publishing Co., 2006

Organic, Shaken and Stirred: Hip Highballs, Modern Martinis, and Other Totally Green Cocktails, by Paul Abercrombie, Harvard Common Press, 2009

Acknowledgments

I am so blessed to have supportive family, friends, colleagues and loyal readers and audiences. Know that all of you are prized and valued beyond measure. My husband, Dan, has my singular thanks for continuing to be my love, rock and most unwavering champion.

Thanks especially to the folks at St. Lynn's Press – Paul Kelly, Cathy Dees, Holly Rosborough and Chloe Wertz – for the special blend of professionalism, talents and kindness that they bring their work. It's been a pleasure, once again.

A special shout out here to the Garden Writers Association and all the helpful people I've connected with through that organization. You have all been instrumental in assisting my growth as a garden communicator, but even more important in sharing your expertise and excitement about plants and gardening with the public at large. May you keep on cultivating the gardening revival.

I lift my glass to you all.

About the Author

C.L. FORNARI is the author of several books, including *Coffee For Roses...and 70 Other Misleading Myths About Backyard Gardening*. Every Saturday, it's her great pleasure to be the host of two call-in radio shows, GardenLine on WXTK and The Garden Lady on WRKO.

C.L. enjoys speaking to a wide variety of audiences, including horticultural groups, professionals at green industry trade shows, and home gardeners. For many years C.L. has run a consultation service at Hyannis Country Garden, a family-owned garden center on Cape Cod. She gardens on Poison Ivy Acres and finds it especially delightful in the growing season when she can walk into the vegetable garden and ask, "What's for dinner?"

On summer evenings C.L. can usually be found on her deck with her husband, Dan. Their cocktail hour ritual is to put gardening tools and digital devices aside, observe the landscape and count their blessings.

OTHER BOOKS FROM ST. LYNN'S PRESS

www.stlynnspress.com

The Right-Size Flower Garden
by Kerry Mendez
160 pages • Hardback
ISBN: 978-0-9892688-7-5

Plants with Benefits
by Helen Yoest
160 pages, Hardback
ISBN: 978-0-9892688-0-6

The 20-30 Something Garden Guide
by Dee Nash
160 pages, Hardback
ISBN: 978-0-9855622-7-4

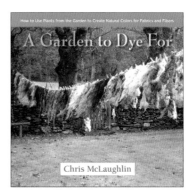

A Garden to Dye For
by Chris McLaughlin
160 pages, Hardback
ISBN: 978-0-9855622-8-1